Ordo Romanus Primus
Latin Text and Translation with Introduction and Notes

Alan Griffiths

Priest of the Roman Catholic Diocese of Portsmouth and a Canon of the Cathedral Lecturer in Liturgy, St John's Seminary, Wonersh.

Contents

The cover picture is a sketch of a typical Roman basilican interior arrangement, based on the pattern of S. Clemente.

First published May 2012
© Alan Griffiths 2012

ISSN 0951-2667
ISBN 978-1-84825-139-7

1

Introduction

The *Ordo Romanus Primus* (ORP hereafter) is the first of a series of medieval documents describing aspects of liturgical practice in the Roman church. It gives details of a papal mass celebrated in the Roman basilica dedicated to the Mother of God on the Esquiline Hill, known now as Santa Maria Maggiore. The occasion was the morning of Easter Day and, although the text of ORP is now found in a largely ninth/tenth century manuscript tradition, it may represent practice as far back as the last decades of the seventh century. Santa Maria Maggiore was the so-called 'station' church for Easter Sunday, 'station' being a term which in the language of the Roman church designated the place appointed for the papal mass on important feasts and fasts.

ORP gives no extended prayer texts, it simply provides a detailed account of the ritual of the mass and the various ministries involved. For so sacred an occasion, this mass may have to modern eyes a rather 'secular' or 'civic' aspect. ORP begins by describing a grand procession of the papal household from the Lateran, the papal residence at that time, to the basilica. Even more strange to our perception of the mass is its description of how, just before the sacred moment of holy communion, papal officials bear invitations to local grandees to dine with the pope after the mass.

ORP describes an elaborate process for gathering the bread and wine for the mass from the people. It details a further complicated process for breaking the consecrated bread (ordinary leavened loaves at this date) and filling the chalices in preparation for holy communion. Like so much else in the description, this is not ceremonial so much as large-scale practical business. ORP is not an account of great ceremonial elaboration for its own sake.

In comparison to this detailed description of rites that must each have taken a significant amount of time to perform, the preface and canon of the mass are very briefly described because they are chanted prayers with, it seems, less of the elaborate signings of the cross and other gestures which the Canon of the mass acquired in its later evolution. The only detail mentioned in the text is that the pope and his archdeacon hold up the consecrated bread and chalice during the doxology at the conclusion of the Canon. Such weighting seems strange to a modern reader for whom it is the Eucharistic Prayer, rather than the preparation of the altar or the communion rites, that is the focus of the celebration.

It seems, though, that the nature of ORP is to be a key to ritual business, not to text. In modern terms, one might describe it as an 'events management' document. Why, then, was it written, and for whom and for what place?

The Context

By the year 1000, most churches in Europe north of the Alps and the Pyrenees were celebrating the mass, the divine office and the sacraments with a core of prayers and liturgical practices derived from the local Church of Rome and its environs. All the medieval so-called 'rites' – Sarum, the Dominican, Carthusian, Carmelite, were basically Roman in character. How had this come about?

Michel Andrieu, the editor of the *Ordines*, prefaced his collection with an introductory essay, telling the story of the spread of the local Roman liturgy into the kingdom of the Franks north of the Alps.[1] It is a fine tale,

---

[1] Michel Andrieu, *Les Ordines Romani Du Haut Moyen Age* (Spicilegium Sacrum Lovanensis, Etudes et Documents Fascicule 23, 5vv., Louvain, 1948). Andrieu prefaced the collection with an introductory essay entitled *La Liturgie Romaine en Pays Franc et Les 'Ordines Romani'*. In referring to geographical areas in this Introduction I have used 'Gaul', 'France', 'the Kingdom of the Franks', 'Italy', etc. It is difficult to be more precise, but the reference is, roughly speaking, to modern France eastward as far as the Rhine and Lombardy, modern Italy south of the Alps.

though more recent studies suggest that many of its details need nuancing.[2] In outline, though, it still provides a general account of the first stages in the process whereby the mass celebrated by the Roman popes of the seventh century eventually became, albeit with significant modifications, the mass we now know worldwide as the Roman Catholic mass.

Andrieu begins his account before 500, when the Church was well established in the Roman Empire of the west. But the Empire collapsed in the fifth/sixth century, and Germanic peoples moved in and settled. All the local churches in former imperial territory suffered from the general instability of the time.

The churches of Gaul and Spain followed their own ancient Latin liturgies, whose origins are not easy to trace. They show affinities with liturgies of North Africa and the Christian East. These liturgies are usually known as the 'Gallican', 'Mozarabic' and 'Ambrosian' rites.[3] In Spain and northern Italy these ancient forms of mass and divine office persisted well into the medieval period. Indeed the Ambrosian rite is still very much alive in the archdiocese of Milan and the Mozarabic rite is reviving, both rites having been subjected to revision and renewal after

---

[2] For example, cf. Yitzhak Hen, *The Royal Patronage of Liturgy in Frankish Gaul* (Henry Bradshaw Society, Subsidia III, London, 2001), for a more recent view of the matter. For an older account see Joseph A. Jungmann SJ, *The Mass of the Roman Rite, its Origins and Development (Missarum Solemnia)*, 2 vols. Tr. Rev. Francis A. Brunner, CSSR, reissued by Christian Classics Inc. (Westminster, Maryland, 1986), vol.1 pp. 67–74 (an account based on ORP) and pp. 74–92.

[3] These are the terms normally used. The 'Gallican' tradition is extinct, and not well understood. English translations of Gallican mass texts are not plentiful. A brief introduction and a single text may be found in R. C. D. Jasper and G. J. Cuming (eds), *Prayers of the Eucharist, Early and Reformed* (3rd ed. rev. and enlarged, Pueblo, New York, 1987) pp.147–149. The 'Mozarabic' (a name used to describe native Iberian Christians under Islamic rule) and 'Ambrosian' (named after Saint Ambrose, Bishop of Milan 367–397) rites are still in use occasionally in Spain and as the normal order of mass and the divine office in the archdiocese of Milan respectively. The liturgical books of both traditions have been extensively revised as part of the liturgical renewal initiated by the Second Vatican Council. There are few translations of texts from these rites, and the most interesting introductions to them are (still) those of Archdale King, cf. his *Notes on the Catholic Liturgie*, (Longmans, Green and Co., London, 1929) and *Liturgies of the Primatial Sees* (Longmans, Green and Co., London, 1957). For the Ambrosian Rite, see also Cesare Alzati, *The Ambrosianum Mysterium*, tr. by George Guiver CR (Alcuin/GROW Joint Liturgical Studies 44 and 47–48 (Grove Books,, Cambridge 1999 and 2000).

the Second Vatican Council.[4] The Gallican tradition does not survive as a living liturgy.

In northern Europe, the Roman liturgy spread partly because of the esteem in which the Roman Church, the church of the apostles Peter and Paul, was held. At the same time, the Roman see was making increasing claims to exercise authority over other churches. As early as the fifth century, the popes were beginning to claim such rights. The letter of Innocent I to Decentius, Bishop of Gubbio. written in 415, was one of the first to commend Roman liturgical customs elsewhere.[5]

Andrieu's Account

Andrieu maintained that the social and political turmoil of the seventh and eighth centuries was the catalyst for the spread of the Roman liturgy. Society in seventh-century France was unstable, as the Merovingian dynasty was weak and Church life suffered as a result.[6] Muslim forces had crossed the Straits of Gibraltar at the beginning of the eighth century and occupied much of the Iberian Peninsula. From there, they proceeded to raid north of the Pyrenees, devastating churches and monasteries, the centres of Christian learning throughout the Languedoc.

The results of this lengthy period of disorder were described bitterly by the English missionary bishop Saint Boniface in 742: no episcopal synods for 24 years; no archbishops or provincial organization, no respect for the rights of the Church; abuses and scandals appearing everywhere. The

---

[4] For an English translation of the 311 Prefaces of the revised Ambrosian Missal, see Alan Griffiths, *We Give You Thanks and Praise, the Ambrosian Eucharistic Prefaces* (Canterbury Press, London, 1999).

[5] See Martin F. Connell, *Church and Worship in Fifth Century Rome, The Letter of Innocent I to Decentius of Gubbio* (Alcuin/GROW Joint Liturgical Studies 52, Grove Books, Cambridge, 2002). Innocent tells us that he sent particles of the sacrament to the presbyters celebrating in the *Tituli* as a sign of mutual communion.

[6] The name 'Merovingian' refers to the royal dynasty of France in the sixth/seventh centuries AD. It is derived from the name Merovech (Latin, Merovius), Father of Childerich, the first king of the Salian Franks. See Richard Fletcher, *The Conversion of Europe From Paganism to Christianity 371–1386 AD* (Harper Collins, London, 1997) p. 102. In the seventh century, a succession of weak kings allowed powerful factions to arise in the kingdom, with corresponding social destabilization.

ancient 'gallican' liturgies seem to have been in a disordered state, or at least what survives of their euchological texts suggests this.

In the eighth century, there seems to have been an attempt to halt the decline in religion. The Merovingian King Childeric III was deposed in 751, the new king, Pepin I, being the father of the great Charlemagne. This new regime had both imperial and evangelistic intentions. Alongside the consequent missionary enterprises among the pagan tribes of northern Europe, measures seem to have been taken for the restoration of church life and clerical discipline.

However, there could be no hope of real improvement without a revival of faith among clergy, monks and the Christian populace. A re-invigoration of the liturgy would be essential for this. As long as clergy were not celebrating the liturgy properly, the ills would persist.

How was a suitable liturgical tradition to be re-established after so much devastation? And how was a liturgical unity to be achieved? The lack of a central authority was a crucial factor in the crisis. While local synods had tried to co-ordinate the actions of bishops and control the lifestyles of priests, in the field of the liturgy they had achieved little.

More recent views

Michel Andrieu's essay has formed the basis of the introduction thus far. While its main lines are generally correct, it might be said that Andrieu's picture is somewhat idealized, even patriotic, being told from a 'French' point of view. His portrayal is that of a European liturgical chaos rescued by a Frankish initiative to romanize the local church, an initiative adopted as an instrument of political policy by the Frankish kings in order to unify their empire.

Nowadays it seems much less clear that that the Frankish imperial regime forced the adoption of one single liturgical standard. While nobody disputes the progress made by the Roman Rite and its growing influence in the Frankish and later Ottonian Empire, it is thought that this progress was slower and the influences underlying it were more varied than simply royal pressure.

Since two of the greatest north European missionary bishops of the eighth century, Saint Boniface and Saint Willibrord, came from England, their influence must be regarded as significant. As told below, it was the liturgy of the Roman rite that took hold in the Anglo-Saxon kingdoms after the mission sent by Gregory the Great to King Ethelbert of Kent in 597.

It is clear also that among the influences which helped the Roman liturgy to spread in northern Europe was that of Benedictine monasticism, itself developing and spreading during the centuries following the appearance of Saint Benedict's seminal *Rule* before 600. The *Rule* lays down a recognizably 'Roman' pattern for the daily liturgical prayer of the monks. The great Benedictine houses of the Frankish kingdom used the Roman liturgy. Benedictine monasticism and the Roman rite of mass seem to go hand in hand.

The Roman Church as Guide

The Roman Church was possessed of apostolic prestige. In the Frankish kingdom, and in England also, *Romanitas* – the Roman, and therefore civilized, values were beginning to be prized in church and state circles. The eighth century produced something of a renaissance in classical learning. The city of Rome, which housed the tombs of the apostles Peter and Paul and countless Christian martyrs, was already a place of pilgrimage. Factors such as these combined eventually to make Roman traditions an inspiration for the liturgy in the Frankish realm and elsewhere in northern Europe. During the residence (753–5) of pope Stephen II in France, King Pepin and some of his bishops came to admire Roman liturgy, chant (more or less a synonym for 'Roman liturgy' since it was all chanted) and ceremonial.[7] The liturgical renaissance entered a decisive phase under Pepin's son Charlemagne. His reign saw a

---

[7] Pope Stephen II and his retinue were the guests of the Frankish King Pepin in 754. See Tom Holland, *Millennium, The End of the World and the Forging of Christendom* (Abacus, London, 2008), pp.23–5.

furtherance of the process whereby the greater Frankish secular churches modelled their liturgy upon that of the Roman Church. However, perhaps a greater, and certainly older, influence came from across the North Sea.

The English Church, founded among the Anglo-Saxon kingdoms with the Gregorian mission of 597, was from its inception firmly within the liturgical orbit of Rome. The Venerable Bede tells us that there were enthusiasts who made sure that it remained so.[8] St. Benedict Biscop (690) was the most famous. Founder of monasteries at Wearmouth (674) and Jarrow (681/2), Benedict made five pilgrimages to Rome and each time brought back quantities of liturgical objects and books.

Benedict found an even more effective means of spreading the practice of the authentic Roman rite in his country. On his fourth journey to Rome he persuaded pope Agatho (672–6) to allow the Roman monk John to come with him to Wearmouth to teach chant and ceremonial. John was the abbot of Saint Martin's monastery, one of four establishments serving the Vatican basilica. He was in fact its principal cantor. John took his mission seriously. He trained disciples who could then celebrate the liturgy 'as they do in Saint Peter's'. Furthermore, he produced many manuscripts. Bede tells us that these were carefully preserved and frequently copied for the generations that followed. His apostolate bore fruit and allowed the liturgy of the Roman Church to put down deep roots in Anglo-Saxon territory.

In the following century, the English Council of Cloveshoo in 747 sought to preserve these traditions unaltered.[9] It decreed that Roman books should be used for the celebration of the mass, for baptism and for the chant on the Sundays of the Church's year. The Roman martyrology was to regulate the cycle of saints' days.

---

[8] See Judith McClure and Roger Collins, *Bede, Ecclesiastical History of the English People, The Greater Chronicle, Bede's Letter to Egbert* (World's Classics Series, Oxford University Press, 1994), pp. 200–1.

[9] The location of the Council is uncertain. One theory is that 'Cloveshoo' is in fact the modern village of Brixworth, Northants, where there is an impressive Saxon church, All Saints, built possibly in the mid-eighth century of recycled Roman materials.

In mainland Europe, Bishop Chrodegang of Metz, sent to Rome in 743, returned with pope Stephen II and on his return began enthusiastically to train his clergy in the Roman liturgical tradition and to follow it himself in his episcopal ministry. Chrodegang introduced at Metz the custom of the 'station mass', an episcopal mass held in different city churches on certain days, just as he had witnessed it in Rome. In the rule he composed for the clerics of his cathedral, Chrodegang commended the practices he had observed in Rome. Carolingian councils increasingly decreed that bishops and priests should celebrate mass and administer baptism according the Roman ritual. Each bishop was directed to open a school in his city where young clerics would be trained in Roman traditions of mass and office. A generation or two later, a priest of Metz, Amalar or Amalarius, would write an exhaustive account of the rites of his Church. It is still a primary source for Roman liturgical history.

The Spread of Roman Liturgical Books

However, it was no mean task to spread the Roman Rite in the territories north of the Alps. An obvious problem was the provision of books.

In our own day, books can be printed in quantities and disseminated easily. The internet is even speedier. In the wake of the Second Vatican Council, Catholics have witnessed how fast liturgical reform takes place, perhaps indeed too fast! Things were quite different before the invention of printing. To transcribe a single volume was a burdensome process, requiring months of work. Copyists did not always copy exactly, many had poor knowledge of Latin. Many could not resist the urge to add material to their copy. So an exact liturgical compliance in the modern sense was never a real possibility, even in the long term.

This was partly because virtually a small library was required to celebrate the liturgy. The first requirement was the Sacramentary, the book used by the priest at the altar, then books for the ministers: the gradual, antiphonary, book of Epistles and book of Gospels, and these just for the mass. For the divine office, the psalter was required, and whole books of both Old and New Testament. Books of responsories and prayers were needed, as would be a lectionary containing the readings from the Fathers, to say nothing of volumes such as the 'legendary' with its lives of martyrs and saints.

For some decades even before 700, liturgical books of the Roman Rite must have already been making their way into Frankish territory. The most important among these was the Sacramentary. This altar book contained the text of the prayers or *orationes* – 'orations' – of the mass. These were the collect, the prayer over the offerings recited after the altar had been prepared and immediately before the Eucharistic Prayer, the Preface or thanksgiving to be chanted at the beginning of the Eucharistic Prayer, the prayer recited after Communion and prayers associated with the dismissal at the end of mass.

These prayers, which changed according to the feast or season, are one of the distinguishing characteristics of the Roman mass. The Sacramentary also contained an outline order of mass and the 'canon,' that is, the fixed portion of the Eucharistic Prayer which followed the chanting of the *Sanctus*. The Sacramentary was a celebrant's book. It did not at first usually contain either readings or chants, these being found in other liturgical books used by other ministers.

Broadly speaking, nineteenth and twentieth century scholarship has classified the surviving Roman Sacramentaries into two types, the first represented by the term 'Gelasian,' after pope Saint Gelasius I (492–6), the second type known collectively as 'Gregorian' being associated traditionally with pope Saint Gregory the Great (590–604). There also exists a collection known today as the Sacramentary of Verona or *Veronense*, which seems to have been compiled about 600 from liturgical prayers contained in the papal archive. It seems not to be a liturgical book so much as what we might call a resource collection of texts.

The 'Gelasian' type is represented by a single manuscript, known as the 'Old Gelasian' currently in the possession of the Vatican library and entered as Vaticanus Reginensis 316.[10] This manuscript was copied, perhaps at the Benedictine convent of Chelles near Paris, about the middle of the eighth century. Behind it lies an older Roman model, which could have been brought to France as much as a century before. The Gelasian Sacramentary seems to have been a liturgical book intended for use in the parish churches of Rome, the so-called *tituli*, which were served by presbyters.

At about the same time as the Old Gelasian was copied, the second type of Sacramentary, the so-called 'Gregorian' seems to have arrived in France.[11] This type of Sacramentary was based on liturgical books used in the major Roman basilicas, rather than the *tituli*. This meant that they were books for mass celebrated by the pope, rather than books for 'parish' liturgy.

A ninth-century manuscript, coming from the Liège region and at present kept in Padua (the so-called *Paduense*), is a copy of a Roman original, possibly used in the Vatican Basilica, which had left Rome before the year 741, possibly even before the end of the seventh century. Between the surviving copy and its ancestor there will have been several intermediate copies, which are now lost.

It seems likely also that other representatives of Roman Sacramentaries had crossed the Alps during the seventh century. Many borrowings from these are found in the Gallican missals that still survive.[12]

Examining these, one can see that Frankish churchmen, without

---

[10] Leo Cunibert Mohlberg OSB, Leo Eizenhofer OSB and Petrus Siffrin OSB (eds), *Liber Sacramentorum Romanae Aeclesiae Ordinis Anni Circuli (Cod. Vat. Reg. lat. 316/Paris Bibl. Nat. 7193, 41/56) (Sacramentarium Gelasianum)* (Casa Editrice, Herder, Rome, 1960). A further earlier collection of mass prayers with the same editors is the *Sacramentarium Veronense (Cod. Bibl. Capit. Veron. LXXXV[80])* (Casa Editrice, Herder, Rome, 1956). Previous generations knew this as the 'Leonine' sacramentary. It seems to be a sort of liturgical resource collection rather than a book for the altar.

[11] Jean Deshusses (ed.), *Le Sacramentaire Gregorien, Ses Principales Formes D'apres Les Plus Anciens Manuscrits*, (3 vols, Editions Universitaires Fribourg Suisse, Fribourg, 1979).

[12] The principal 'Gallican' Sacramentaries accessible in modern editions. Leo Cunibert Mohlberg OSB, Leo Eizenhofer OSB and Petrus Siffrin OSB(eds), *Missale Francorum (Cod. Vat. Reg. Lat. 257)*, (Casa Editrice, Herder, Rome, 1957); Leo Cunibert Mohlberg OSB, Leo Eizenhofer OSB and Petrus Siffrin OSB (eds), *Missale Gallicanum Vetus (Cod. Vat. Palat. Lat. 493)* (Casa Editrice, Herder, Rome, 1958), which also contains the so-called *masses of Mone*, another early Gallican collection of mass texts; Leo Cunibert Mohlberg OSB (ed.), *Missale Gothicum (Vat. Reg. Lat. 317)* (Casa Editrice, Herder, Rome, 1961).

abandoning the traditional shape of the Gallican mass, had introduced into it many prayers from the Roman Sacramentaries. In place of the many variable Eucharistic Prayers typical of the Gallican rite, the single Roman 'canon' was evidently becoming a popular option. These borrowings seem to come from both the Gelasian and Gregorian types of sacramentary.

The importation of Roman books into France seems at first to have been a private initiative. Pilgrim monks or clerics wanted to celebrate the holy sacrifice as they had done at the tombs of the apostles. They had, therefore, to obtain one or other of the Sacramentaries which they used in the Holy City. If they possessed the resources of a Benedict Biscop they might acquire the books themselves, or else they might have copies made.

Such was the situation about the year 750. Among those who celebrated according to Roman usage, both Roman 'types' of Sacramentary, the Gelasian and Gregorian were in use. Also, Gallican and Roman prayers existed side by side.

A first attempt at unifying liturgical practice seems to have taken place in mid- century. From this period a new Sacramentary type appears, merging the two Roman types. The name usually given to this type of compilation is that of 'eighth-century Gelasian'.

Festivals proper to each of the preceding types were retained. For the overall plan of the book, the Gregorian type serves as a model. That is to say, the masses of the proper of seasons, the proper of saints and the votive masses, were arranged in a single series instead of being divided into three separate books as the Gelasian Sacramentary had been. The order of mass, however, was that of the Gelasian, with its orations and often a proper preface. The Gelasian provided the rituals for baptism, ordination, marriage, the reconciliation of penitents, funerals and so on. The eighth century Gelasians proved popular. Some dozen exemplars survive.[13]

In the later years of the eighth century, the Emperor Charlemagne

---

[13] The two best are known as the Sacramentary of Gellone, published in A Dumas-J. Deshusses (eds), *Liber Sacramentorum Gellonensis, textus n.664*, (Corpus Christianorum Series Latina 159, Brepols, Turnhout, 1981); and the Sacramentary of Angouleme published in P. St Roch (ed.), *Liber Sacramentorum Engolismensis (Cod. B.N. Lat.816)*, n.650 (Corpus Christianorum Series Latina 159C, Brepols, Turnhout, 1987).

sought and obtained an authentic copy of the Roman Sacramentary from pope Hadrian I. This, the pope said, was the book which the Roman Church had received from Saint Gregory the Great.

However, the volume which Charlemagne received, known today as the *Hadrianum*, or the 'Gregorian of Hadrian' proved unsatisfactory. It had been prepared for the personal use of the pope on those days when he went to celebrate the station mass in one of the Roman basilicas. Effectively, this meant that provision was made for the season of Lent and the Sundays in Christmastide, Eastertide, together with a number of important Roman festivals. Consequently, it was incomplete. It would not serve as a book for mass throughout the year.

Charlemagne employed a Benedictine monk, Benedict of Aniane, to compile a 'Supplement' to complete it.[14] Benedict drew heavily on the eighth-century Gelasian Sacramentary type. Interestingly, he also included elements of 'Gallican' practice.

In general, the Gallican liturgy, in some of its rituals such as ordinations, blessings of religious, dedication of churches and so on, was much more elaborate than was the sober, business-like, Roman liturgy. Its more dramatic rites appealed more to the imagination. Pastorally, it would have been an impoverishment to give all that up.

Benedict's 'Supplement' gave these local traditions generous space. It included a number of blessings: the *Exsultet* for blessing the Paschal candle at the Easter Vigil, blessings for altars and sacred vessels, clothing for virgins and widows and above all, votive masses, masses for the dead and for many different intentions.

The Gelasian Sacramentaries of the eighth century also continued in use and in some places were still being copied in the eleventh century. However, little by little, the liturgical books were evolving into collections of texts that synthesized material from both Roman Sacramentary traditions.

---

[14] This supplement, known as *Huiusque* ('thus far ..') from its opening word, was formerly thought by some liturgical historians to be the work of the Anglo-Saxon scholar Alcuin of York, cf. J. A. Jungmann SJ, cited above n.2, p. 63.

The lineage of the *Hadrianum* developed from the bipartite Sacramentary and *Supplementum* into a more integrated liturgical book. Its contents remained intact in each of its descendants and survived without significant alteration into the beginnings of the development of what we know as the 'missal' around the turn of the millennium. Now equipped with readings and chants, the missal nevertheless retained a more or less direct lineage from the book sent to Charlemagne by pope Hadrian and revised by Benedict of Aniane.

In medieval Europe, a variety of missals proliferated. Though all 'Roman' at their core, they differed in details, depending on the diocese or province. In England the most popular was the missal of Salisbury, or 'Sarum' missal.[15] In Rome, the Papal court, the Curia, developed its own missal. On this was based the missal of the Franciscan Order and, eventually, the *Missale Romanum* of 1570 produced following the Council of Trent. This in turn was basically the missal in use for most of the Catholic Church until the reforms mandated by the Second Vatican Council.

The Need for a Ceremonial Handbook

Books were one thing. But liturgy is much more than books. Whenever a Frankish priest returned from Rome carrying a Roman Sacramentary with the idea of introducing its use in his monastery or church, 'doing things as they do in Rome', he would have encountered a problem, 'doing what exactly?' The texts of the Sacramentaries lacked any detailed rubrics or ritual context. Again, he could receive training in the Roman chant, but how would the various pieces fit into a celebration of mass? Furthermore, there was the practical business to be considered. How was the bread and wine to be prepared? How were the consecrated gifts to be made ready for Holy Communion? How should ministerial functions be allotted?

---

[15] The Sarum missal text, at various stages of its development, has appeared in various editions. The earlier MS tradition is in J. Wickham Legg (ed.), *The Sarum Missal edited from Three Early Manuscripts* (The Clarendon Press, Oxford, 1916).

The *Ordines Romani* seem to have been intended at first as the answer to that question. Some 40 of these survive. The earlier ones at least purport to describe mass celebrated in Rome by the pope. However, some of them seem to represent circumstances that were not those of the Roman basilicas where the pope celebrated mass.

This is not surprising, as they seem not to have been intended as museum-pieces or wish-lists but as practical handbooks. If they originate in notes taken down in Rome, then their repeated copying for use north of the Alps seems to have introduced accommodations to local custom. However enthusiastic the churchmen may have been for the Roman liturgy, they knew that prudence always meant a measure of compromise with their own local traditions.

Two instances of this may be found by comparing the *Ordo Romanus Primus* with later *ordines*.

The first of these addresses an issue that is once again a matter of debate in the Catholic liturgy today, that of 'orientation'. Should the priest celebrate the liturgy of the Eucharist *versus populum*, facing the people across the altar, or should he stand *ad orientem* in front of the altar, facing the same direction as the people he is leading in prayer?[16]

In Gaul, as in the eastern churches, it was customary for both priest and people to face east for prayer and to orient church buildings towards the east. However, in Rome, the Papal basilicas were not oriented like this. In Saint Peter's, for example, to face east is to face the main entrance. In modern terms, by facing east, the pope faced down the nave of the basilica across the altar. This is the layout that is described in ORP, where also the papal chair is in the apse behind the altar. However, in later *ordines* the chair has moved to its Gallican position to the right of the altar and the celebrant faces the same way as the people for the most sacred part of the rite. These later *ordines* also record that the space in the

---

[16] After more than a generation of 'mass facing the people' as the preferred liturgical option, the question of the orientation of liturgical prayer and the Eucharistic Prayer in particular has been taken up again in recent years, cf. U. M. Lang, *Turning towards the Lord, Orientation in Liturgical Prayer* (Ignatius Press, San Francisco, 2004).

apse vacated as a result of this move was taken up during part of the mass by the choir and at other times by the seven candlesticks carried by the acolytes before the pope.

A second instance concerns the elevation of the bread and chalice at the conclusion of the Canon of the mass. In ORP, the pope and his archdeacon hold up the bread and the chalice respectively during the whole of the doxology *Per ipsum et cum ipso et in ipso* – 'Through him and with him and in him ...' This seems to be the only elevation in the canon, as the raising of the host after the words of consecration did not appear until several hundred years later. ORP seems to take this doxological elevation as a sacrificial gesture, the prayer of offering concluding and climaxing with the appropriate gesture of uplifting the holy gifts. Later *ordines*, however, reduce the gesture. The elevation is only at the doxology's concluding words, *omnis honor et gloria*. This became the practice which remained the norm until the reform of the Roman missal under pope Paul VI.

Subsequent *ordines* continue to show a process of adaptation from a local Roman setting to a Frankish one and in liturgical scale, from a papal to an episcopal mass, and so on. The *ordines* are, in fact, the precursors of the rubrics which came to proliferate in the medieval missals, and, ultimately, of the General Instruction on the Roman Missal after Vatican II.

The Organization of the Roman Church

ORP gives us a picture of the way the local church of Rome was organized and how its various degrees of ministry functioned. 'Degrees' is an accurate term, since ministry seems to be regarded as a ladder, with the pope at its summit.

Whereas one might expect nowadays that priests would play a signifi-cant role in the Roman Church, it is surprising how little they feature in the mass described in ORP. In fact, what ORP records is the importance of the diaconate as an upper management tier and beneath this, the sub-diaconate as the lower, working, tier of management. Acolytes and others come lower again, but each degree seems to have its particular liturgical function. Deacons, for instance, are associated both with the chanting of the Gospel and the administration of the chalice at mass.

ORP shows ecclesiastical Rome as being divided into seven regions, each under the care of a deacon, under whom regional sub-deacons operated. Priests took charge of those churches of the city, the so-called *tituli*, which were effectively the parish churches, as opposed to the patriarchal basilicas connected especially with the pope. The origins of some of the *tituli* were ancient, linking the developed episcopal system of the Roman Church with an earlier, pre-Constantinian phase when a single episcopal authority was less in evidence.

The term 'station' has already been mentioned as the name given to those churches where the pope's mass was to be said on certain days. In pre-Vatican II editions of the Roman missal, certain masses during the year were given the title 'station at Saint X' meaning that the church in question hosted a mass which was, nominally at least, *the* liturgy of the Roman Church for that day. The pope was also accompanied by what we might now call 'lay' officials, though these were likely to be in lower grades of ministry or 'minor orders'. The papal 'household' and its economic administration had undergone significant reorganization under Gregory the Great, a development which reflected the pope's growing importance as the senior civic official of the city.

ORP also tells us that the influence of the local Roman Church extended to the local bishoprics, the towns in the Roman area, whose bishops appear to have been present alongside the pope. It illustrates how the idea of eucharistic communion between churches within the city may have at one time been ritually expressed by the taking of a small portion of the consecrated bread to parish churches or *tituli* whose priests could not be at the papal mass because they were celebrating for their own people.

Date of the *Ordo Romanus Primus*

Though the manuscript tradition of ORP is ninth/tenth century, the actual date of the tradition which it describes is older than this. It seems that the organization of the Roman Church and the papal household referred to in the document in part reflects ancient practice and in part some of the reforms of Saint Gregory the Great. However, the most important pointer to this dating is the fact that during the mass at the breaking of the loaves, the chant known today as the *Agnus Dei* 'Lamb of God' – a litanic formula – was sung.

Roman sources record that this chant was introduced into the mass at the end of the seventh century by pope Sergius I: 'He laid down that at the breaking of the Lord's Body, "Lamb of God who take away the sins of the world" should be sung by the clergy and people.'

Sergius' family background was originally in Palestine, and this chant is one of the two in the Roman liturgy to be addressed to Christ (the other being the *Kyrie eleison* at the beginning of the mass, though this was lost sight of in the later Middle Ages, as the many medieval tropes to the *Kyrie* demonstrate). Such address was more common in the east, and this particular usage of using the term 'Lamb of God' in connection with the consecrated loaves at the eucharist is certainly eastern. Sergius may also have been registering a protest at a decree of a Council known as the Council in Trullo (692) which forbade the representation of Christ as a lamb.[17]

It seems that ORP is contemporary with these events. This suggests a date somewhere in the last years of the seventh century.

As to the location of the mass, In ORP this is the basilica of Santa Maria Maggiore on the Esquiline Hill, founded in the fifth century in honour of the Council of Ephesus' definition of the Blessed Virgin Mary as *Theotokos*, God-bearer, or Mother of God. To this day, and unlike its counterparts at the Lateran (refashioned in the seventeenth century) and Saint Peter's (completely rebuilt in the sixteenth/seventeenth centuries), Santa Maria Maggiore retains something of the feel of

---

[17] See L. Duchesne (ed.), *Le Liber Pontificalis* (2 vols, Paris, 1886–92) vol. 1 p. 376., and *ibid.*, *Origines Du Culte Chrétien* (5me ed., Paris, 1920) p.158. See also Joseph A. Jungmann SJ, cited above, n. 2. vol. 1 p. 74.

the sixth/seventh-century basilica in its mosaics and general interior aspect.

The procession forms early in the morning, even though, unlike some other Roman Churches, Santa Maria Maggiore is not that far from the Lateran. The name of the road, the Via Merulana, which connects the two buildings, remains the same even today. The procession carries with it the books, vestments and sacred vessels to be used at the mass, all taken from the pope's treasury.

Importance of the Ordo

ORP is important as an historical witness. To understand the purpose of ORP and subsequent *ordines* as instruments for the establishment of Roman style liturgy in Frankish churches offers an insight into the ritual development of the mass at a time of change and adaptation. This liturgy shows us, for the first time, the beginnings of a trajectory of liturgical development which will eventually culminate in the *Missale Romanum* of the Council of Trent.

However, the importance of ORP is more than simply historical. Starting with the work of Edmund Bishop and Anton Baumstark in the early part of last century, modern liturgical studies have broadened the field from an older focus on texts and their development.[18] A recognition that the liturgy is primarily something done, has led to a greater interest in liturgical practice and ritual. The religious, historical and social interpretation of ritual has also excited new interest in recent years.[19]

Also important in this connection is the interest in Liturgy as *Theologia*

---

[18] Edmund Bishop's essay 'The Genius of the Roman Rite' may be found in his *Studia Liturgica* (The Clarendon Press, Oxford, 1918), pp.1–19. For an introduction to Baumstark, see Fritz West, *The Comparative Liturgy of Anton Baumstak* (Alcuin/ GROW Joint Liturgical Studies 31, Grove Books, Bramcote, Nottingham, 1995).

[19] Cf. Richard D. McCall, *Liturgy As Performance* (University of Notre Dame Press, Notre Dame, Indiana, 2007). A similar approach may be found in Martin D. Stringer, *A Sociological History of Christian Worship* (The University Press, Cambridge, 2005).

Prima – 'first level theology'.[20] Taking its starting point from the remark of Prosper of Aquitaine ... *ut legem credendi lex statuat supplicandi*, that the rule of liturgical prayer should found the law of believing, this school of liturgical and theological study reads accounts such as ORP with the greatest interest.[21] If liturgy is church and faith 'on the move', and if liturgy is to faith what language is to being human, then accounts such as ORP are of the highest interest not merely from a ritual point of view but as theological documents.

An examination of the text as a unique record will suggest much about the more detailed theological implications in the action of the rite. ORP offers a fascinating testimony to a ritual practice which predates the controversies over the meaning of the Eucharist and in particular the notion of the relationship between the eucharistic bread and cup and the Lord's sacrifice of his body and blood, something which occupied minds from the ninth century and ultimately came to fruition in the developed idea of 'transubstantiation' and the definitions of the Fourth Lateran Council in 1215.

To instance this, a reading of the provisions for the preparation of the 'consecrated' bread and wine for holy communion will raise questions as to whether all the wine collected at the offertory and used to supplement the chalices for the giving of holy communion was regarded as 'consecrated' in the post-medieval sense, or even whether such a question may be put at all. One student remarked to me on the volume of 'consecrated crumbs' that the breaking of the bread in ORP would inevitably produce. Surely, this would be a serious problem for a generation of priests accustomed to the unleavened 'hosts' we customarily use, to say nothing of the spillage of wine. ORP is evidently not for the scrupulous.

---

[20] This is the theme of David Fagerberg, *Theologia Prima, What is Liturgical Theology?* (Liturgy Training Publications, Archdiocese of Chicago, 2004), and of Aidan Kavanagh OSB, *On Liturgical Theology* (Pueblo, New York, 1984), particularly pp. 73–121.

[21] Cf. P. De Letter, *Prosper of Aquitaine, Defense of Saint Augustine* (Ancient Christian Writers vol.xxxii, Westminster MD, 1963), p. 183.

Conclusion

ORP is a fascinating document. In describing the solemn mass of the Roman Church, it offers a portrait of the city of Rome some two centuries after the collapse of the Empire. It testifies to the ascendancy of the pope as both a religious and civic leader. It originates in a city whose religious authority was growing even though its political importance had long since declined. It allows a glimpse of an event that is both of God and of the human city. It gives us a first look at how the established customs of the local Roman mass were to spread into the new Frankish realms to the north and in that journey to be transformed. For the modern reader it raises interesting questions as to how sacredness was perceived and sacred things dealt with. In these and many other ways it is surely worthy of study.

Translation of the *Ordo Romanus Primus*

Ordo Romanus Primus exists in a number of manuscript versions. Andrieu's edition remains the standard. Printed English translations are by C. F. Atchley in 1905 and in Jasper/Cuming.[22]

Both Atchley's and Cuming's versions are unsatisfactory in different ways. Atchley's version is written in a high Victorian English. Students nowadays find this English (let alone the Latin original) almost impossible to understand. Jasper and Cuming's translation is incomplete. For this translation I have used the text in Andrieu, the 'standard' edition of the text, which is based on a wider manuscript collation than the one available to Atchley.

Andrieu's edition takes account of the great number of variant

---

[22] Cuthbert F. Atchley, L. R. C. P., M. R. C. S., *Ordo Romanus Primus, With Introduction and Notes* (The Library of Liturgiology & Ecclesiology for English Readers, Vol. vi, Alexander Moring Limited, The De La More Presss, London, 1905). For the incomplete modern translation see R. C. D. Jasper and G. Cuming, *Prayers of the Eucharist, Early and Reformed* (3rd ed. rev. and enlarged, Pueblo, New York, 1987). For another partial translation based on Atchley and co-ordinated with contemporary liturgical texts, see McCall, n.19 above, pp. 137–59. McCall also prints excerpts from the later *Ordo iv* known to Atchley as the *Ordo of Saint Amand.*

readings in the MS. Sometimes these amount to significant additions to the text, which nonetheless do not add greatly to its understanding. Sometimes they make for difficult reading. Since my intention has been to produce a translation for the non-specialist with no knowledge of Latin, for whom the inclusion of such variants would be of limited interest, I have therefore tended to leave them out. However, I have included some of the more important variants where I thought – arbitrarily perhaps – that points of ceremonial needed inclusion or clarification.

Following Andrieu, I have used for this translation principally the ninth century manuscript known as Sangallensis, the oldest known MS of this document. In Andrieu's edition, the first 23 paragraphs, which describe the procession of the pope to the stational church from the Lateran Palace, have been taken from other MSS. I have followed the numbering of paragraphs used by Andrieu. The MS tradition is highly complex with hundreds of variant readings. I have not included the bulk of these, as for the most part these are of interest to the specialist rather than the ordinary reader. Where they seem to be important, I have included them.

The Latin text I have used is printed in the left-hand columns. It is based upon Andrieu's text, and represents the most credible reading I could establish. It is there not to stimulate detailed textual criticism or to exhibit all possible variant readings, but simply to authenticate the translation which accompanies it. Andrieu will provide the complications for the specialist scholar; my purpose has been to equip students with less grasp of Latin with an accurate running text in translation. I hope that readers with Latin will be able almost at sight to understand the principles on which I have translated the text.

2

Latin Text and Translation

Incipit ordo ecclesiastici ministerii romanae ecclesiae vel qualiter missa caelebratur.

This is the organization of ministers in the Roman Church, and how the mass is celebrated.

1. Primum omnium observandum est septem esse regiones ecclesiastici ordinis urbis Romae et unaquaeque regio singulos habere diacones regionarios.

First of all, it should be observed that for ecclesiastical purposes the city of Rome is divided into seven districts and each district has one district deacon.[1]

2. Et uniuscuiusque regionis acolyti per manum subdiaconi

2. The acolytes of each district are under the authority of the district

---

[1] The organization of the Roman Church into seven districts each managed by a deacon is ancient. It testifies to the importance of the diaconate and the high profile given to its role in managing the Church's charitable works.

regionarii diacono regionis suae officii causa subduntur.

deacon, by reason of his office, and managed by the district sub-deacon.

3. Quorum diaconorum si quando quispiam moritur, donec loco eius alius subrogetur, illius regionis acolyti archidiacono oboediunt, quia omnes acolyti, cuiuscumque regionis sunt, causa ecclesiastici officii ad ministerium eius pertinent.

3. Should the district deacon die, the acolytes of that district come under the archdeacon until another deacon is chosen to replace him, for all acolytes of whatever district come under his management by virtue of his office.

4. Quod etiam de sequentibus ordinibus intelligendum est, servata unicuique post eum proprii gradus archidiaconi in sui ordinis ministerio subditis, ut si quis, verbi gratia, vim passus fuerit sive ab ecclesiastico seu a quacumque militari persona, si a sui ordinis primo eius causa ad effectum minime pervenerit, habeat archidiaconus, id est vicarius pontificis, causam, qualiter subditorum sibi quaerelas absque notitia possit explicare pontificis; caetera vero per minores ordines finiantur.

4. As regards the other orders, it should be understood that each minister occupies his own proper rank in exercising his ministry under the authority of the archdeacon. So, for instance, should anyone sustain an injury from an ecclesiastic or lay person, and the case cannot be settled by the senior of his own order, the archdeacon as the pope's vicar-general should take the matter up, since he has the authority to deal with the complaints of those under his authority without having to consult the pope.[2] Other matters are to be determined by the lesser orders.

---

[2] The Latin throughout ORP for the pope is pontifex. This was the ancient pagan term for the senior priest of the state religion, who also had the job of keeping the bridges (pontes) over the Tiber (a sacred river) in good repair. The popes simply took it over. I have rendered it by 'pope' as being the more recognizable term nowadays.

5. Nam primo scire oportet, ut, post numerum ecclesiasticarum regionum, sciat, qui voluerit, numerum dierum per ebdomadem, quo ordine circulariter obsequantur: nam prima feria regio tertia, id est paschae, secunda feria regio quarta, tertia feria regio quinta, feria quarta regio sexta, feria quinta regio septima, feria sexta regio prima, sabbato regio secunda ordines proprios tam in processione quam in ecclesia, vel ubicumque eos propria dies ratione sui gradus prisca statutio ire vel ministrare conpulerit, a ministerio pontificis non poterit sine ulla sui deesse excommunicationis vel animadversionis sententia disciplinae.

5. Firstly, in order to understand how the number of the ecclesiastical districts and the number of the days of the week correspond, one needs to know what order they follow. On the first day of the week, Easter in this case, the third district is responsible.[3] On Monday, it is the fourth district; on Tuesday, the fifth district; the sixth on Wednesday; the seventh on Thursday; on Friday the first district is responsible; and on Saturday the second. Each district, then, will take its proper place in procession and in church, or wherever a particular day obliges them to assemble or minister because of its rank. This is all according to ancient constitution. The district clergy may not be absent from attending on the pope without incurring sentence of excommunication or censure.

6. Quorum ministeria primitus secundum rationem simplicem

6. They used to divide this attendance into two parts by a simple

---

[3] The mass described in ORP is that of Easter Sunday. The system of 'station masses' took the pope to the Roman basilicas and intramural parish churches for mass daily during Lent and at other times in the Church's year. A 'station' (statio in Latin) originally meant a halt on a march. On Easter Sunday the mass was held at Santa Maria Maggiore, the basilica constructed in the fifth century after the Council of Ephesus in honour of the Mother of God. It must have been a liturgy attended by substantial numbers of people, because the arrangements for the offertory and communion are so elaborate. It is characteristic of Roman liturgical culture, however, that the ceremoniousness of these actions is not solely for the sake of drama or any sort of symbolism. It is a practical ritual. There is a lot of bread and wine used.

dupliciter diebus singulis dividuntur, id est in processione apostolici ad stationem et in egressu sacrarii usque ad missarum consummationem.

rule of thumb; first, attendance at the apostolic procession to the stational church and second, from the point where they leave the sacristy until the end of mass.

7. Diebus itaque sollemnibus, id est pascha, primo omnes acolyti regionis tertiae et defensores omnium regionum convenientes diluculo in patriarchio Lateranensi praecedunt pontificem pedestres ad stationem.

7. Thus on solemn feast days (Easter in this case), all the acolytes of the third district and the counsellors of every district assemble early in the morning at the papal residence, the Lateran, and proceed on foot in front of the pope to the stational church.

8. Stratores autem laici a dextris et a sinistris equi ambulant ne alicubi titubet.

8. Lay grooms walk on the right and left of his horse in case it should stumble anywhere.[4]

9. Qui autem eum equitantes praecedunt, hii sunt: diacones, primicerius et duo notarii regionarii, defensores regionarii, subdiaconi regionarii. Procedunt vero divisis turmis, spatium inter se et apostolicum facientes.

9. The following ride on horseback in front of the pope: the deacons, the chancellor and the two district notaries, the district counsellors, and the district subdeacons. They proceed in two groups with a space between them and the pope.

10. Post equum vero hi sunt qui equitant: vicedominus, vesterarius, nomincolator atque sacellarius.

10. The following ride after the (pope's) horse: the pope's vicar, the sacristan, the secretary and the treasurer.

---

[4] The papal household after Gregory the Great was predominantly clerical. As a former monk, Saint Gregory did not want non-clerics waiting on him. He felt that the papal household should be a model of religious community life.

11. Unus autem ex acolytis stationariis praecedit pedester equum pontificis gestans sanctum chrisma manu in mappula involuta cum ampulla. Sed et omnes acolyti absque sacculis et syndones et chrismate non procedunt, quod disponit stationarius.

11. One of the acolytes from the stational church walks in front of the pope's horse, carrying in his hand the sacred chrism in its vessel wrapped in a cloth. The remaining acolytes carry sacks, linen cloths and chrism and walk in the procession. The official in charge of the station church will organize this.

12. Si quis autem adire voluerit pontificem, si equitat, statim ut eum viderit, discendit de equo et ex latere viae expectat, usquedum ab eo possit audiri.

12. If anyone desires access to the pope, he must dismount if on horseback as soon as he sees him coming, and wait by the roadside until he can be heard by him.

13. Et, petita ab eo benedictione, discutitur a nominculatore vel sacellario causa eius et ipsi indicant pontifici et finiunt; quod etiam observabitur etiamsi absque ulla petitione ei quisquam obvius fuerit.

13. After he has sought a blessing from him, his case will be reviewed by the secretary or treasurer, and they shall state it briefly to the pope and make a determination. This is also the procedure should anyone come before him (the pope) even if he has no petition.

14. Qui vero pedester fuerit, tantummodo loco suo figitur, ut ab eo audiatur vel benedicatur.

14. If a petitioner is on foot, he stays where he is so that he may be heard and blessed by him (the pope).

15. Die autem resurrectionis dominicae, procedente eo ad Sanctam Mariam, notarius regionarius

15. On the day of the Lord's resurrection, as the pope goes to Saint Mary Major, the district notary will

stat in loco qui dicitur Merolanas et, salutato pontifice, dicit: 'In nomine domini nostri Iesu Christi, baptizati sunt hesterna nocte in sancta Dei genetrice Maria infantes masculi numero tanti, feminae tantae.' Respondit pontifex: 'Deo gratias'. Et accepit a sacellario solidum unum; pontifex autem pergit ad stationem.

be standing at the place known as *Ad Merulanas*.[5] After greeting the pope he says: 'In the name of our Lord Jesus Christ, last night in the church of Saint Mary the holy Mother of God, there were baptized x number of baby boys and girls'. [6] The pope answers 'Thanks be to God'. The notary receives from the treasurer the sum of one solidus. The pope continues on his way to the stational church.

16. Feria secunda, ad remissa similiter.

16. A similar procedure takes place on the Monday.

17. Feria tertia, in reflexione portici sancti Pauli tantum item qui pedestres absequuntur.

17. On the Tuesday, in the porch of Saint Paul's, only those who are on foot attend.

18. In diem vero sanctum paschae, omnes acolyti regionis tertiae simul et defensores omnium regionum conveniunt primo diluculo in patriarchio Lateranensi, ut, dum processerit pontifex, equum illius praecedant.

18. However, on the day of holy Pascha, all the acolytes of the third district together with the counsellors of every district meet at the Lateran residence at daybreak, so that when the pope sets out they may go in front of his horse.

19. Acolyti autem, qui inde fuerint, observant ut portent chrisma ante

19. The acolytes who come from there take care to carry the chrism,

---

[5] The modern street that links Santa Maria Maggiore to the Lateran basilica is still known as the Via Merulana.

[6] This is, presumably, a reference to the Paschal Vigil. By the late seventh century, adult baptisms had died out but children were brought for baptism.

pontificem et evangelia, sindones et sacculos et aquamanus post eum, sicut supra diximus.

the gospel book, cloths, sacks and basins behind (the pope) as we said above.

20. Apostolum autem subdiaconus qui lecturus est sub cura sua habebit, evangelium archidiaconus.

20. The subdeacon who is to read the epistle (Apostolum) should carry the Epistle Book and the archdeacon should look after the Gospel Book.

21. Aquamanus, patena cottidiana, calicem, sciffos et pugillares et alios aureos et gemelliones argenteos, colatorio argenteo et aureo et alio maiore argenteo, amas argenteas, cantatorio et caetera vasa aurea et argentea, cereostata aurea et argentea de ecclesia Salvatoris per manum primi mansionarii sumunt et baiuli portant.

21. The hand-basins, the daily paten, the chalice, the bowls and the reeds of gold and the silver vessels with the gold and silver strainer and another larger one of silver, the chant book and other gold and silver vessels, the gold and silver candlesticks from the church of the Saviour are issued by the chief sextons and carried by bearers.

22. Diebus vero festis, calicem et patenam maiores et evangelia maiora de vestiario dominico exeunt sub sigillo vesterarii per numerum gemmarum, ut non perdantur.

22. On feast days the larger chalice and paten and the larger gospel book are issued from the papal sacristy under the sacristan's seal on account of being decorated with quantities of gems, lest these be lost.[7]

23. Sellam pontificis cubicularius

23. The lay chamberlain goes on

---

[7] It looks as if all the things needed for mass were brought along with the papal entourage. The turbulence of the times meant that precious goods were frequently looted, something which regularly occurred after the death of a pope, for example. The vessels themselves may have been large. ORP says at one point that the paten had to be slung in a cloth tied around the subdeacon's neck. This indicates a large and bulky tray rather than the small disc we know as a paten today.

laicus praecedens deportat, ut parata sit dum in sacrario venerit.]

ahead carrying the pope's portable chair so that it may be there when he arrives in the sacristy.

[In Andrieu's edition, nos. 1–23 form part of what is known as the Long Recension of the Ordo. The rest, which describes the mass at the station church, follows below as nos.24–125.]

24. Ordo romane ecclesie denuntiatione statutis diebus festis.

Prima mane praecedit omnis clerus apostolicum ad ecclesiam ubi statio antea fuerit denuntiata, exceptis his qui in obsequio illius comitantur ut supra diximus, et expectantes pontificem in ecclesia cum supplementario et baiulis et reliquis qui cruces portant, sedentes in presbiterio, episcopi quidem ad sinistram intrantibus, presbiteri vero in dexteram, ut, quando pontifex sederit, ad eos respiciens, episcopos ad dexteram sui, presbiteros vero ad sinistram contueatur.

24. The order of the Roman Church for the stational mass on feast days.

Early in the morning, all the clergy go on ahead of the pope to the church where it had previously been announced that the station mass was to take place. Those who are to await him in church do not go. They are: the almoner and the bearers who carry the crosses sitting in the presbytered area. The bishops enter on the left-hand side, the presbyters on the right, so that when the pope is seated and looks toward them, he will see the bishops on his right and the presbyters on his left.

25. At vero pontifice iuxta ecclesiam veniente, exeuntes acolyti et defensores ex regione illa cuius dies

25. When the pope arrives at the church, the acolytes and counsellors of that district whose day of

ad officium venerit in obsequium prestulantes eum in loco statuto, antequam veniat ubi discensurus a sella eius.

duty it is, go to meet him at the appointed place before he reaches the place where he gets down from his chair.

26. Similiter et presbiter tituli vel ecclesiae ubi statio fuerit, una cum maioribus domus ecclesiae romanae, vel pater diaconiae, si tamen illa ecclesia diaconiae fuerit, cum subdito sibi presbitero et mansionario tymiamaterium deferentibus in obsequium illius inclinato capite dum venerit.

26. Similarly, the presbyter of the 'titulus' or church where the station mass is to be held, together with the major-domos of the Roman church, or else the 'Father', if that church is a 'diaconia', together with the presbyter subordinate to him, and the sexton, carring a thurible out of respect for the pope.[8] When he arrives, they all bow their heads.

27. Primum acoliti cum defensoribus, deinde presbiteri cum suis, petita benedictione, divisis hinc inde partibus, prout militant, praecedunt pontificem usque ad ecclesiam.

27. The acolytes with the counsellors, and the presbyters with those accompanying them, having asked for a blessing, divide into groups on either side as their service requires and walk in front of the pope into the church.

28. Advocatores autem ecclesiae stant quidem cum maioribus, non autem praecedunt cum eis, sed ipsi

28. But the advocates of the church, although they are standing with the major-domos, do not go in the

---

[8] A 'titulus' was, in effect, a Roman parish church within the city walls. The name came from Roman property ownership. A house would be officially known as the 'titulus Plauti' after Plautus (say) its owner. Before the fourth century, the churches of Rome met in large houses, often adapted for the purpose. Some of these were the origin of the 'tituli' and their owner's name sometimes transformed itself into a saint's name. The Church of Santa Cecilia in Trastevere was anciently the 'Titulus Caeciliae' after its owner, who may or may not have been a martyr. Other churches were known as 'diaconiae' because they were connected with charitable work (like the modern US 'pantry' associated with churches).

tantummodo sequuntur sellarem pontificis cum acolyto qui aquamanus portat, quem semper necesse est sequi pontificem, usquedum ad altare ascendit, paratus sub humero in presbiterio, quando vocetur a subdiacono regionario ad aquam dandam.

procession with them. They simply follow the pope's chair along with the acolyte who carries the bowl for washing the pope's hands. He must always wait upon the pope until he goes up to the altar, and be ready at his elbow in the presbyteral are to be called forward by the district subdeacon to offer water.[9]

29. Cum vero ecclesiam introierit pontifex, non ascendit continuo ad altare sed prius intrat in secretario, sustentatus a diaconibus, qui eum susceperint de sellario descendentem, ubi, dum intraverit, sedet in sella sua et diaconi, salutato pontifice, egrediuntur secretario et ante fores eiusdem mutant vestimenta sua.

29. Now when the pope enters the church, he does not proceed directly to the altar but first enters the sacristy, supported by deacons who held him as he left his chair. The deacons, after greeting the pope, leave the sacristy to change their robes in front of its doors.

30. Et parat evangelium qui lecturus est; reserato sigillo, ex praecepto archidiaconi, super planetam acolyti, tenente eo, parat evangelium.

30. The reader of the gospel prepares the gospel book. The seal being opened at the archdeacon's orders, an acolyte holds the book for him outside his chasuble, and he finds the place for the gospel reading.[10]

---

[9] ORP gives some hints as to the layout of a Roman church at this time. The best known surviving example is the basilica of San Clemente, with its enclosed area in the middle of the nave with raised ambos on either side for the readings and chants, an apse raised above nave level with papal cathedra in the apse and the altar under its ciborium or canopy at the front. One should probably add to that the sort of open screen still found in, for instance, Santa Maria in Cosmedin, dividing the people's part of the building from that of the clergy. Men and women were separated on different sides of the building.

31. Quo facto, acolytus defert evangelium usque ante altare in presbiterio, precedente eum subdiacono sequente, qui, eum de super planeta illius suscipiens, manibus suis honorifice super altare ponat.

31. When this has been done, the acolyte carries the book to the altar in the presbyteral area, preceded by the subdeacon in attendance. He takes the book from the acolyte's chasuble and reverently places it upon the altar.

32. Nam, egredientibus diaconibus de secretario, remanent cum pontifice primicerius, secundicerius, primicerius defensorum, notarii regionarii, defensores regionarii, subdiaconi et subdiaconus sequens, qui tenet pallium pontificis in brachio suo super planeta in sinistro brachio cum acus.

32. After the deacons have left the sacristy, the chancellor, the secretary, the chief counsellor, the district notaries, subdeacons and subdeacon attendant remain with the pope. The subdeacon attendant holds the pope's pallium and its pins over his left arm outside his chasuble.

33. Pontifex autem per manus subdiaconorum regionariorum mutat vestimenta sollemnia hoc ordine: defert ea plicata cubicularius tonsoratus, accepta a manibus ostiarii, iuxta caput scamni, subdiacono regionario.

33. The pope now changes into his vestments for the mass with the help of the district subdeacons, in this way. The chamberlain-cleric, having received them from the doorkeeper, brings them to the bench for vesting.

---

[10] ORP tells us that the chasuble was worn by clergy generally, not just by priests as nowadays. Before the 1962 revision of the Roman missal, in penitential seasons the deacon and subdeacon at high mass wore chasubles folded up the front. This is the descendant of the clothing described in ORP. The chasuble was a large bell-shaped cloak, and often one grasped sacred objects such as the gospel book through it, a posture displayed in some contemporary mosaics. Alb, tunic and chasuble were the normal Roman secular dress of the time. There is a famous portrait of Gregory the Great standing with his mother and father. They are all identically dressed in albs, tunics, dalmatics and chasubles. Gregory's pallium and decorated slippers are all that mark him out as a priest.

34. Et tunc ceteri subdiaconi regionarii secundum ordinem suum accipiunt ad induendum pontificem ipsa vestimenta, alius lineam, alius cingulum, alius anagolaium, id est amictum, alius lineam dalmaticam et alius maiorem dalmaticam et alius planetam et sic per ordinem induunt pontificem.

34. The remainder of the district subdeacons take the vestments for vesting the pope in order of rank: first the alb, then another brings the cincture, then the amice, then the linen dalmatic. Another brings the larger dalmatic and another the chasuble.[11] Thus they vest the pope in order.

35. Primicerius autem et secundicerius componunt vestimenta eius, ut bene sedeant.

35. The chancellor and the secretary arrange the vestments so that they hang properly.

36. Novissime autem quem voluerit domnus pontifex de diaconibus vel subdiaconibus, cui ipse iusserit, sumit de manu subdiaconi sequentis pallium et induit super pontificem et configit eum cum acus in planeta retro et ante et in humero sinistro et salutat domno, dicit: 'Iube, domne, benedicere'. Respondet: 'Salvet nos dominus'. Respondet: 'Amen'.

36. Lastly, the deacon chosen by the lord pope, or one of the subdeacons whom he may designate, takes the pallium from the subdeacon attendant and places it around the pope's shoulders, fastening it to the chasuble with the pins at the back and front and on the left shoulder. He salutes the lord pope saying: 'A blessing, my lord'. The pope replies: 'The Lord save us', and he replies: 'Amen'.

37. Deinde subdiaconus regionarius, tenens mappulam pontificis in sinistro brachio super planetam

37. Then the district subdeacon who holds the pope's maniple over his left arm above his unfolded

---

[11] These were still the pontifical vestments until the Vatican II reforms. Note also that the stole is not mentioned. This seems to have been an import from Gallican/Spanish practice. All bishops wore the pallium, until it became a mark of archiepiscopal rank or a papal honour later on in the middle ages.

revolutam, exiens ad regiam secretarii, dicit: 'Scola'. Respondet: 'Adsum'. Et ille: 'Quis psallit?' Respondet: 'Ille et ille'.

chasuble goes to the entrance and says: 'Choir!' They answer: 'Present'. He says: 'Who is to sing?' They answer: 'X and Y'.

38. Et rediens ad pontificem subdiaconus porrigit ei mappulam, inclinans se ad genua ipsius, dicens: 'Servi domini mei talis subdiaconus regionarius legit apostolum et talis de scola cantat'.

38. Returning to the pope, the subdeacon offers him the maniple, kneeling before his knee saying: 'My lord's servant, the district subdeacon, is to read the epistle and XY from the choir is to sing'.

39. Et iam non licet alterum mutare in loco lectoris vel cantoris. Quod si factum fuerit, archiparafonista a pontifice excommunicabitur, id est quartus scolae, qui semper pontifici nuntiat de cantoribus.

39. From now on, no changes are to be made to readers or cantors. If changes are made, the 'fourth of the schola', who informs the pope on singers' matters, is to be excommunicated by the pope.

40. Qui dum nuntiatum fuerit, statim sequitur quartus scolae subdiaconus, adstans ante faciem pontificis, usquedum ei annuat pontifex ut psallant; cui dum annuerit, statim egreditur ante fores secretarii et dicit: 'Accendite'.

40. When this has been announced, the 'fourth of the schola' and the subdeacon in attendance stand before the pope until he signals him to start the singing. When the order is given, he immediately goes to the sacristy doors and says: 'Light up!'

41. Qui cum incenderint, statim subdiaconus sequens, tenens tymiamaterium aureum, pro foribus ponit incensum, ut pergat ante pontificem.

41. When the candles have been lit, the attendant subdeacon, who holds the golden censer, at once puts incense into it outside the sacristy doors so that he may walk in front of the pope.

42. Et ille quartus scolae pervenit in presbiterio ad priorem scolae, vel secundum sive tertium, inclinato capite, dicit: 'Domne, iubete'.

42. The 'fourth of the schola' goes up to the presbyteral area to the choir director, or one of his assistants, nods to him and says: 'Sir, give the order!'

43. Tunc illi, elevantes per ordinem, vadunt ante altare; statuuntur per ordinem acies duae tantum iuxta ordinem, parafonistae quidem hinc inde a foris, infantes ab utroque latere infra per ordinem.

43. Then they go up and pass in order before the altar. They position themselves in two groups with the seniors of the schola on either side before the gate of the presbyteral area, and the choirboys inside.

44. Et mox incipit prior scolae antiphonam ad introitum, quorum vocem diaconi dum audierint, continuo intrant ad pontificem in secretarium.

44. Now the leader of the schola begins the introit antiphon. Hearing them singing, the deacons enter the sacristy and go to the pope.

45. Et tunc pontifex elevans se dat manum dexteram archidiacono et sinistram secundo, vel qui fuerit in ordine: et illi, osculatis manibus ipsius, procedunt cum ipso sustenantes eum.

45. Then the pope rises, gives his right hand to the archdeacon and his left to the second deacon, or whoever is in line. They kiss his hand and move off, supporting him.

46. Tunc subdiaconus sequens cum tymiamaterio praecedit ante ipsum, mittens incensum, et septem acolyti illius regionis cuius dies fuerit, portantes septem cereostata accensa praecedunt

46. The subdeacon in attendance walks in front of him with the censer, wafting the incense and the seven district acolytes whose day's turn it is carry the seven lighted candlesticks. They walk in front

ante pontificem usque ante altare.

of the pope up to the altar.

47. Diaconi vero, priusquam veniant ante altare, infra presbiterio exuunt se planetis et suscipit eas subdiaconus regionarius et porrigit illas ad acolytos regionis cuius fuerint diaconi.

47. Before the deacons get to the altar, they remove their chasubles in the presbyteral area. The district subdeacon takes these and gives them to the acolytes of the deacons' districts.

48. Et tunc duo acolyti, tenentes capsas cum Sancta apertas, et subdiaconus sequens cum ipsis tenens manum suam in ore capsae ostendit Sancta pontifici vel diacono qui processerit. Tunc, inclinato capite, pontifex vel diaconus salutat Sancta et contemplatur ut, si fuerit superabundans, praecipiat ut ponatur in conditorio.

48. Then two acolytes approach, holding open pyxes containing the holy sacrament. The subdeacon in attendance takes them, holding them by the rim of the pyx and shows the sacrament to the pope or to the deacon who precedes him. Then the pope or deacon venerate the sacrament with a bow of the head and he inspects it, so that if there are too many fragments he will direct that they be placed in the vessel for reservation.[12]

49. Tunc peraccedens, antequam veniat ad scolam, dividuntur cereostata, quattuor ad dexteram et tres ad sinistram et pertransit pontifex in caput scolae et inclinat caput ad altare, surgens et orans et faciens crucem in fronte sua, et dat

49. The pope continues in procession, but before he comes to the choir, the candlebearers divide, four to the right and three to the left. The pope passes through them to the upper part of the schola area and bows his head towards the

---

[12] The significance of this is not clear. It might be that the reserved sacrament is being inspected to see if it is fresh, or possibly, it is being checked to see that the particle which the pope will place in the chalice after the canon of the mass is sufficient.

pacem uni episcopo de ebdo-
madariis et archipresbitero et diaconibus omnibus.

altar. Then he rises, prays and
makes the sign of the cross on his
forehead and gives the sign of
peace to one of the hebdomadary
bishops, to the archpresbyter and
the deacons.

50. Et respiciens ad priorem scolae
annuit ei ut dicat 'Gloriam'; et
prior scolae inclinat se pontifici et
inponit. Quartus vero scolae praecedit ante pontificem, ut ponat or-
atorium ante altare; et accedens
pontifex orat super ipsum usque
ad repetitionem versus.

50. Then, turning towards the
schola leader, he signals him to sing
'Glory be to the Father...' The
leader bows to the pope and begins
it. The 'fourth of the schola' goes in
front of the pope to place his fald-
stool in front of the altar. The pope
comes up and prays at it until the
verse (the antiphon) is repeated.

51. Nam diaconi surgunt quando
dicit: 'Sicut erat', ut salutent altaris
latera, prius duo et duo vicissim
redeuntes ad pontificem. Et surgens pontifex osculat evangelia et
altare et accedit ad sedem et stat
versus ad orientem.

51. When the schola are singing 'As
it was...' the deacons go up to
venerate the altar at the sides, before returning, two by two, to the
pope. He rises, kisses the gospel
book and altar and goes to his seat,
to stand facing the east.[13]

52. Scola vero, finite antiphona, inponit 'Kyrie eleison'. Et continuo
acoliti ponunt cereostata in pavi-
mento ecclesiae, tres quidem in
dexteram partem et tres in sinistram, unum vero in medio, in spa-
tio quod est inter eos. Prior vero

52. When the antiphon is finished,
the schola begins to sing 'Kyrie eleison'. Then the acolytes place their
candlesticks on the church floor,
three on the right and three on the
left and one in the middle in the
space between them. The schola

---

[13] See the Introduction (p. 17 above) concerning the orientation of the liturgy in ORP.

scolae custodit ad pontificem, ut ei annuat quando vult mutare numerum laetaniae et inclinat se pontifici.

leader keeps his eye on the pope, so that the pope may indicate to him when he wants to alter the number of the litanies, and he bows to the pope.

53. Quando vero finierint, dirigens se pontifex contra populum incipit 'Gloria in excelsis Deo' si tempus fuerit. Et statim regerat se ad orientem usquedum finiatur. Post hoc dirigens se iterum ad populum dicens: 'Pax vobis', et regerans se ad orientem dicit: 'Oremus', et sequitur oratio. Post finitam sedit. Similiter episcopi vel presbiteri sedent.

53. When they have finished, the pope turns to the people and begins 'Glory to God in the highest', if it is the season for it. He turns to face east immediately until they have finished. Then he turns to face the people again and says 'Peace be with you' and turning east again he says 'Let us pray' and the prayer. At the conclusion of the prayer he sits down. Bishops and presbyters also sit.

54. Et tunc tolluntur cereostata de loco in quo prius steterant, ut ponantur in una linea per mediam ecclesiam. Interea diaconi, si tempus fuerit, levant planetas in scapulas et stant iuxta pontificem; similiter et levant subdiaconi, sed cum sinu.

54. And then they pick up the candlesticks from where they had previously been standing, so as to place them in a line across the middle of the church. Meanwhile the deacons, if it is the season, lift their chasubles onto their shoulders and stand next to the pope. Subdeacons do likewise, but fold theirs.

55. Et tunc ascendunt subdiaconi regionarii ad altare, statuentes se ad dexteram sive sinistram altaris.

55. The district subdeacons go up to the altar and take up positions to its right and left.

56. Subdiaconus vero qui lecturus

56. Now when the subdeacon who

est, mox ut viderit post pontificem episcopos vel presbiteros resedentes, ascendit in ambonem et legit.

57. Deinde ascendit alius cum cantatorio, dicit responsum. Deinde alius 'Alleluia'.

58. Ad completionem autem 'Alleluia' vel responsorii, parant se diaconi ad evangelium legendum. Si autem diaconus ibidem non fuerit, presbiter sicut diaconus stat iuxta pontificem, sed non relevata planeta; at, ubi evangelium legere debet, ibi se parat ubi et diaconus. Sed statim ubi perlegerit evangelium et venerit ante altare, revestit planeta et ornat altare sicut diaconus.

59. Deinde diaconus osculans pedes pontificis et tacite dicit ei pontifex: 'Dominus sit in corde tuo et in labiis tuis'. Deinde venit ante altare et, osculatis evangeliis, levat in manus suas codicem et procedunt ante ipsum duo subdiaconi regionarii levantes tymiamaterium de manu subdiaconi sequentis, mittentes incensum, et ante se habentes duos acolytos portantes

is to read sees the pope and the bishops and presbyters take their seats, he climbs up into the ambo and reads the epistle.

57. Then another minister goes up with the chant book and sings the responsory, and another, the alleluia.

58. At the ending of the 'Alleluia' or the responsory, the deacons prepare to read the gospel. However if a deacon is not present, a presbyter, like a deacon, stands by the pope, only without removing his chasuble. Then as the deacon would, he prepares himself in the place where the gospel is to be read. But as soon as he has read the gospel and returned before the altar he puts on the chasuble again and venerates the altar as a deacon would.

59. Then the deacon kisses the pope's feet and the pope says quietly to him: 'May the Lord be in your heart and on your lips'. Then he comes before the altar, kisses the gospel book and takes it up in his hands. Two district subdeacons go in procession in front of him, they take the censer from the subdeacon in attendance and waft the incense smoke. They have two acolytes in

duo cereostata; venientes ad ambonem dividuntur ipsi acolyti ut per medium eorum subdiaconi et diaconi cum evangelio transeant.

front of them carrying two candlesticks. When they reach the ambo, the acolytes step aside to allow the subdeacon and deacon to pass through.

60. Et cum transierit cum evangelia ante episcopos inclinans se ad eos, illi dant ei benedictionem ita: 'Dominus tecum'. Post haec, inclinat se ad presbiteros et illi dicunt: 'Spiritus domini super te'.

60. And when he crosses with the book of gospels in front of the bishops he bows to them and they give him this blessing: 'The Lord be with you'. After that he bows to the presbyters and they say: 'The Spirit of the Lord be upon you'.

61. Ille vero subdiaconus qui absque timiamaterio est, vertens se ad diaconem porrigit ei brachium suum sinistrum, in quo ponit evangelium, ut manu subdiaconi aperiatur ei locus in quo signum lectionis positum fuerit.

61. The subdeacon, who is not carrying the censer, turns to the deacon and puts out his left arm on which he lays the gospel book, so that the subdeacon may open it with his right hand at the place where the reading was marked.

62. Et, interposito digito suo, diaconus in loco lectionis ascendit ad legendum et illi duo subdiaconi redeunt stare ante gradum discensionis ambonis.

62. Then, slipping his finger into the page where he is to begin reading, the deacon goes up to read. The two subdeacons return to stand in front of the steps to the ambo.

63. Finito evangelio, dicit pontifex: 'Pax tibi'. Deinde dicit: 'Dominus vobiscum'. Resp.: 'Et cum spiritu tuo'. Et dicit: 'Oremus'.

63. When the gospel is finished, the pope says: 'Peace be with you'. And then: 'The Lord be with you'. They reply: 'And with your spirit'. And he says: 'Let us pray'.

64. Descendente autem diacono, subdiaconus qui prius aperuerat, recipit evangelium et porrigit eum subdiacono sequenti, qui in filo stat; quod tenens ante pectus suum super planetam porrigit osculandum omnibus per ordinem graduum qui steterint.

64. As the deacon descends from the ambo the subdeacon, who earlier had opened the book takes the gospel book, and gives it to the subdeacon in attendance who is standing in line. Holding the book in front of his chest over his chasuble, he offers it to be kissed by all in order.

65. Deinde ponitur in capsa, ut sigilletur, et ab acolito eiusdem regionis cuius subdiaconus est reportatur ad locum suum.

65. Then it is put in a case to be locked and taken back to its place by an acolyte from the same district as the subdeacon.

66. Ceteri vero accoliti sumentes cereostata ponent ea retro altare per ordinem.

66. The other acolytes take up the candlesticks and place them in a line behind the altar.

67. Deinde, pergente diacono ad altare, veniens acolytus cum calice et corporale super eum, levat calicem in brachio suo sinistro et porrigit diacono corporalem, ut accipiat de super calicem, et ponit eum super altare a dextris, proiecto capite altero ad diaconem secundum ut expandant.

67. Then, a deacon goes to the altar and an acolyte comes forward with the chalice and on top of it, the corporal. Raising the chalice in his left hand, he offers the corporal to the deacon to take off the chalice and spread upon the altar at the right hand end. He throws the other end of the corporal to a second deacon, so that they may spread it out.[14]

68. Tunc ascendunt ad sedem primicerius et secundicerius et

68. Then the chancellor and the secretary, the chief counsellor, the dis-

---

[14] The corporal is obviously not of the postage stamp size commonly used today, but a large tablecloth.

primicerius defensorum, cum omnibus regionariis et notariis; subdiaconus vero cum calice vacuo sequitur archidiacono.

trict officials and notaries, all go up to the pope's seat. The subdeacon with the empty chalice follows the deacon.

69. Pontifex autem postquam dicit 'Oremus', statim descendit ad senatorium, tenente manum eius dexteram primicerio notariorum et primicerio defensorum sinistram, et suscipit oblationes principum per ordinem archium.

69. Having said: 'Let us pray', the pope immediately goes down to the senatorial area, with the chancellor holding his right hand and the chief counsellor his left and he receives the oblations of the principal citizens in order of seniority.[15]

70. Archidiaconus post eum suscipit amulas et refundit in calice maiore, tenente eum subdiacono regionario, quem sequitur cum sciffo super planetam acolytus, in quo calix impletus refunditur.

70. Behind him, the archdeacon receives the flasks of wine and pours them into the large chalice held by the district subdeacon. An acolyte follows, holding a bowl over his chasuble, into which the chalice is emptied when it becomes full.[16]

71. Oblationes a pontifice suscipit subdiaconus regionarius et porrigit subdiacono sequenti et subdia-

71. A district subdeacon receives the loaves from the pope and hands them to the subdeacon in at-

---

[15] The term *oblationes*, 'offerings' clearly means 'loaves' and I have translated it accordingly. The context suggests that they are leavened bread, presented by at least some of the congregation. Extant images of mass from this period show them as small round buns, a bit like those still used in some eastern rites. The use of a sheet to carry them suggests that there is a great deal of bread involved. Altars were not large and there is a prayer over the offerings for St. John the Baptist's day in the 1962 missal which graphically illustrates the scene: 'We heap up your altar, Lord, with offerings'.

[16] The ritual is to fill the chalice, which will be the only wine vessel actually placed on the altar. Then, each time this chalice is filled from the small flasks of wine brought by the people, its contents are emptied into bowls. We have to assume that these are retained near the altar, possibly by acolytes, during the canon of the mass.

conus sequens ponit in sindone quam tenent duo acolyti.

tendance, who places them in a linen sheet carried by two acolytes.

72. Reliquas oblationes post pontificem suscipit episcopus ebdomadarius, ut ipse manu sua mittat eas in sindone qui eum sequitur.

72. After the pope, the hebdomadary bishop receives the remainder of the loaves and places them in the sheet that follows him.[17]

73. Post quem diaconus, qui sequitur post archidiaconem, suscipit amulas et manu sua refundit in sciffum.

73. After him, a deacon, receives the flasks of wine and pours them into the bowl, after the archdeacon.

74. Pontifex vero, antequam transeat in partem mulierum, descendit ante confessionem et suscipit oblatas primicerii et secundicerii et primicerii defensorum; nam in diebus festis post diacones ad altare offerunt.

74. The pope, before crossing over to the women's side of the church, comes down in front of the *confessio* and there receives the loaves of the chancellor, secretary and chief counsellor, for on feast days they make their offering at the altar after the deacons.[18]

75. Similiter ascendens pontifex in parte feminarum et complet superscriptum ordinem.

75. Likewise, the pope goes to the women's area and follows the same procedure.

76. Similiter et presbiteri si necesse fuerit post eum vel in presbiterio faciunt. Post hoc pontifex, tenente

76. If necessary, the presbyters do the same, either after the pope or within the presbyteral area. After

---

[17] The Hebdomadary (from the word for 'weekly') bishops and presbyters are those to whom the daily liturgical ministry is entrusted.

[18] The confessio or 'confession' is the sunken space in front of the altar where saints' relics are kept.

ei manum primicerio et se-cundicerio, reddit ad sedem suam, abluit manus suas.

this, the pope, with the chancellor and the secretary supporting him by the hand, returns to the seat and washes his hands.

77. Archidiaconus stans ante altare, expleta susceptione, lavat manus suas; deinde respicit in faciem pontificis, at ille annuit ei et ille resalutato accedit ad altare.

77. Now that the taking up of the offerings has been completed, the archdeacon stands before the altar and washes his hands. He faces the pope who nods to him. He returns the nod and so comes up to the altar.

78. Tunc subdiaconi regionarii, levantes oblatas de manu subdiaconi sequentis super brachia sua, porrigunt archidiacono et ille componit altare; nam subdiaconi hinc inde porrigunt.

78. Then the district subdeacons collect the offerings from the subdeacon in attendance and give them to the archdeacon. He arranges them on the altar, since the subdeacons are presenting them from each side of it.

79. Ornato vero altare, tunc archidiaconus sumit amulam pontificis de subdiacono oblationario et refundit super colum in calicem, deinde diaconorum et in die festo primicerii, secundicerii defensorum.

79. When the altar is prepared, the archdeacon takes the pope's flask from the subdeacon 'oblationer' and pours it through a strainer into the chalice. Then he does the same with the flasks brought by the deacons and on feast days by the chancellor, secretary and chief counsellor.

80. Deinde descendit subdiaconos sequens in scola, accipit fontem de manu archiparafonistae et defert archidiacono et ille infun-

80. Then the subdeacon in attendance goes down to the choir area and receives the ewer of water from the senior singer and brings it to the

dit, faciens crucem, in calicem.

archdeacon. He pours it into the chalice, making the sign of the cross.

81. Tunc ascendunt diaconi ad pontificem; quos videntes primicerius, secundicerius et primicerius defensorum regionariorum et notarii regionarii et defensores regionarii descendunt de aciebus, ut stent in loco suo.

81. Then the deacons go up to the pope. Seeing them approach, the chancellor, the secretary and the district chief counsellor, the district notaries and counsellors go down from their positions to occupy their proper places.

82. Tunc surgit pontifex a sede, descendit ad altare et salutat altare et suscipit oblatas de manu presbiteri ebdomadarii et diaconorum.

82. Then the pope rises from his seat and goes down to the altar. He venerates it and receives loaves from the hebdomadary presbyter and deacons.

83. Deinde archidiaconus suscipit oblatas pontificis de oblationario et dat pontifici.

83. Then the archdeacon receives the pope's loaves from the 'oblationer' and gives them to the pope.

84. Quas dum posuerit pontifex in altare, levat archidiaconus calicem de manu subdiaconi regionarii et ponit eum super altare iuxta oblatam pontificis ad dextris, involutis ansis cum offerturio, quem ponit in cornu altaris, et stat post pontificem.

84. When the pope has placed these on the altar, the archdeacon takes the chalice from the district subdeacon and places it on the altar to the right of the pope's loaves, with the offertory veil around the handles. He lays the veil on the corner of the altar and takes his place behind the pope.

85. Et pontifex, inclinans se paululum ad altare, respicit scolam et annuit ut sileant.

85. The pope makes a slight bow to the altar, looks over to the schola and signals them to stop singing.

86. Tunc, finito offertorio, episcopi sunt stantes post pontificem, primus in medio, deinde per ordinem, et archidiaconus a dextris episcoporum, secundus diaconus a sinistris et ceteri per ordinem disposita acie.

86. The offertory is now complete. The bishops are in position behind the pope, the senior in the middle, the rest according to rank. The archdeacon stands to the right of the bishops, the second deacon to the left, the others arranged according to rank.

87. Et subdiaconi regionarii, finito offertorio, vadunt retro altare, aspicientes ad pontificem, ut quando dixerit 'Per omnia secula', aut 'Dominus vobiscum', aut 'Sursum corda', aut 'Gratias agamus', ipsi sint parati ad respondendum, stantes erecti usquedum incipiant dicere hymnum angelicum, id est 'Sanctus, Sanctus, Sanctus'.

87. The district subdeacons go to the other side of the altar when the offertory is at an end, and stand facing the pope, so that when he says: 'For ever and ever', 'The Lord be with you', 'Lift up your hearts' and: 'Let us give thanks ...', they will be ready to make the responses. They stand upright until they begin singing the angelic hymn: 'Holy, Holy, Holy...'

88. Ut autem expleverint, surgit pontifex solus in canone; episcopi vero, presbiteri, diaconi, subdiaconi permanent inclinati.

88. When they have finished this hymn, the pontiff alone rises for the canon, while the bishops, presbyters and deacons remain bowed.[19]

89. Et cum dixerit: 'Nobis quoque peccatoribus', surgunt subdiaconi; cum dixerit: 'Per quem haec omnia, domine', surgit archidi-

89. And when he has said: 'To us also, sinners', the subdeacons rise. When he has said: 'Through whom, Lord, you create all these

---

[19] The pope alone recites the canon after the Sanctus. Other ordines tell us that on some days, the bishops recited it quietly with the pope, as in a modern concelebrated mass.

aconus solus; cum dixerit: 'Per ipsum et cum ipso', levat cum offertorio calicem per ansas et tenet exaltans illum iuxta pontificem.

good things ...' the archdeacon alone rises; when he says: 'Through him and with him', the archdeacon lifts up the chalice by the handles with the offertory veil and holds it up, towards the pope.

90. Pontifex autem tangit a latere calicem cum oblatis, dicens: 'Per ipsum et cum ipso', usque: 'Per omnia saecula saeculorum', et ponit oblationes in loco suo et archidiaconus calicem iuxta eas, dimisso offerturio in ansas eiusdem.

90. The pope touches the side of the chalice with the loaves and says: 'Through him and with him and in him,' to 'for ever and ever', and puts the loaves back in their place. The archdeacon places the chalice next to them.

91. Nam quod intermisimus de patena, quando inchoat canonem, venit acolytus sub humero habens sindonem in collo ligatam, tenens patenam ante pectus suum in parte dextera usque medium canonem.

91. We have left out some details about the paten. When the pope begins the canon, an acolyte comes up behind him with a sheet tied at the neck holding the paten in front of his chest by the right hand side until the middle of the canon.[20]

92. Tunc subdiaconus sequens suscipit eam super planetam et venit ante altare, expectans quando eam suscipiat subdiaconus regionarius.

92. Then the subdeacon in attendance receives the paten over his chasuble and comes before the altar, waiting for the district subdeacon to receive it.

---

[20] Andrieu quotes Amalarius of Metz, who says that 'the middle of the canon' means the Te igitur, that is, the part immediately following the Sanctus. The canon was understood as beginning with the Sursum corda: 'Lift up your hearts.'

93. Finito vero canone, subdiaconus regionarius stat cum patena post archidiaconem.

93. When the canon is finished, the district subdeacon stands with the paten behind the archdeacon.

94. Quando dixerit: 'et ab omni peturbatione securi', vertit se archidiaconus et osculatam patenam dat eam tenendam diacono secundo.

94. When the pope says: 'and safe from all disquiet', the archdeacon turns, kisses the paten and gives it to the second deacon to hold.

95. Cum vero dixerit: 'Pax domini sit semper vobiscum', faciens crucem tribus vicibus manu sua super calicem mittit Sancta in eum.

95. When the pope has said: 'The peace of the Lord be with you always', he makes three signs of the cross over the chalice, [he places a portion of the sacrament in the chalice[21]].

96. Archidiaconus vero dat pacem priori episcopo, deinde ceteri per ordinem et populus similiter.

96. The archdeacon gives the sign of peace to the senior bishop, then the rest do so in order; the people do likewise.

97. Tum pontifex rumpit oblatam ex latere dextro et particulam quam ruperit partem super altare relinquit; reliquas vero oblationes suas ponit in patenam quam tenet diaconus.

97. Then the pope breaks a piece from the right hand of the loaf and leaves the broken fragment on the altar. The rest of his loaf he places on the paten which the deacon is holding.

---

[21] This seems to be the fragment of the sacrament from a previous mass, mentioned earlier as being inspected by the pope as he comes into the church. Andrieu comments that this may be a relic of the practice known as the *fermentum*. The pope sent particles of the sacrament from his mass to the masses being celebrated in the other churches of Rome, for their priests to place in the chalice as a mark of communion with him. A further commixture follows after the pope receives communion.

98. Pontifex vero statim ascendit ad sedem suam. Mox primicerius et secundicerius et primicerius defensorum cum omnibus regionariis et notariis ascendunt ad altare et stant ad dextris et sinistris.

98. Then straightaway he goes up to his seat. Immediately the chancellor, secretary and chief counsellor together with all the district officials and notaries, go up to the altar and stand in order to right and left.

99. Nomincolator vero et sacellarius et notarius vicedomini, cum dixerint, 'Agnus Dei', tunc ascendunt adstare ante faciem pontificis, ut annuat eis scribere nomina eorum qui invitandi sunt sive ad mensam pontificis per nomincolatorem, sive ad vicemdomini per notarium ipsius; quorum nomina ut conpleverint, descendunt ad invitandum.

99. The 'invitationer' and the treasurer and the notary of the pope's vicar go up to face the pope while the schola is singing the Agnus Dei, so that he may signal to them to write down names of those to be invited to the pope's table by the 'invitationer' or to that of the pope's vicar, by his notary. When the list is complete they go down to deliver the invitations.

100. Nam archidiaconus adprehendit calicem de super altare, dat eum subdiacono regionario et tenet iuxta cornu altaris dextrum usquedum confrangantur oblationes.

100. The archdeacon takes the chalice from the altar and gives it to a district subdeacon. He keeps hold of it at the right hand side of the altar until the loaves have been broken.

101. Et accedentes subdiaconi sequentes cum acolytis qui saccula portant a dextris et a sinistris altaris, extendentibus acolytis brachia cum sacculis, stant subdiaconi sequentes ab utroque cornu altaris, parant sinus sacculorum

101. The subdeacons in attendance now come forward to the right and left of the altar, with the acolytes who carry little sacks. The acolytes hold out their arms with the sacks and the subdeacons in attendance stand at each corner of the altar.

archidiacono ad ponendas oblationes, prius a dextris, deinde a sinistris.

They turn the opening of the sacks
towards the archdeacon for him to
put the loaves inside, first on the
right, then on the left.

102. Tunc acolyti vadunt dextra
levaque per episcopos circum
altare; reliqui descendunt ad presbiteros, ut confrangant hostias.

102. Then the acolytes go to right
and left, along the line of bishops
round the altar. The rest go down
to the presbyters, so that they may
break the hosts.

103. Patena praecedit iuxta sedem,
deferentibus eam duobus subdiaconibus regionariis diaconibus ad
frangendum.

103. The paten, carried by two district subdeacons, goes to the
(pope's) seat, so that the breaking
of the bread may begin.

104. At illi aspiciunt ad faciem
pontificis, ut eis annuat frangere; et
dum eis annuerit, resalutato pontifice, confringunt.

104. They look towards the pope,
for him to signal them to break the
loaves. They return the pope's signal and break the loaves.

105. Et archidiaconus, evacuato
altare oblationibus, preter particulam quam pontifex de propria
oblatione confracta super altare
reliquid, quia ita observant, ut,
dum missarum solemnia peragun-
tur, altare sine sacrificio non sit,
respicit in scolam et annuit eis ut
dicant 'Agnus Dei' et vadit ad patenam cum ceteris.

105. Once the altar has been
cleared of the loaves, except for the
fragment which the pope himself
broke off his own loaf and left on
the altar (they do this so that, while
the mass is being celebrated, the
altar should not be without the
sacrifice) the archdeacon looks
over to the schola and gives the signal for them to sing: 'Lamb of
God...' Then he goes to the paten
with the rest.

106. Expleta confractione, diaconus minor, levata de subdiacono patena, defert ad sedem, ut communicet pontifex.

106. When the breaking has been completed, the second deacon takes the paten from the subdeacon and takes it to the seat so that the pope may receive communion.

107. Qui, dum communicaverit, ipsam particulam de qua momorderat, consignando tribus vicibus, mittit in calicem in manus archidiaconi. Et ita confirmatur ab archidiacono.

107. When he has received, he places the particle from which he had bitten into the chalice held by the archdeacon, making the sign of the cross three times. Then he receives communion from the chalice from the archdeacon.[22]

108. Deinde venit archidiaconus cum calice ad cornu altaris et adnuntiat stationem ita: 'Illo die veniente, statio erit ad sanctum Illum, foras aut intus civitate'. Resp.: 'Deo gratias' et refuso parum de calice in sciffo inter manus acolyti, accedunt primum episcopi ad sedem, ut communicent de manu pontificis secundum ordinem.

108. Then, the archdeacon comes with the chalice to the corner of the altar, and announces the (next) station mass thus: 'on N day forthcoming, the station will be at Saint N., outside or within the city'. Response: 'Thanks be to God.' Then, when he has poured a little from the chalice into the bowl held by the acolyte, the bishops come up first to the seat, that they may receive communion from the pope in order.

109. Sed et presbiteri omnes ascendunt ut communicent ad altare.

109. All the presbyters also come up to receive communion.

---

[22] The verb used for 'give communion from the chalice' throughout ORP is the single word 'confirmat', which suggests the sense that the chalice 'completes the communion'.

110. Episcopus autem primus accipit calicem de manu archidiaconi et stat in cornu altaris confirmat sequentes ordines usque ad primicerium defensorum.

110. The senior bishop takes the chalice from the archdeacon and positions himself at the corner of the altar. He gives the chalice to the other orders down to the chief counsellor.

111. Deinde archidiaconus, accepto de manu illius calice, refundit in sciffum quem supra diximus et tradit calicem subdiacono regionario, qui tradit ei pugillarem cum quo confirmat populum.

111. Then the archdeacon takes the chalice from him and pours its contents into the bowl we mentioned above. He gives the chalice to the district subdeacon, who passes to him the reed used for the communion of the people.[23]

112. Calicem autem accipit subdiaconus sequens, dat acolyto, ab illo revocatur in paratorio.

112. The subdeacon in attendance receives the chalice and gives it to an acolyte, and it is replaced by him in the sacristy.

113. Qui dum confirmaverit, id est quos papa communicat, descendit pontifex a sede, cum primicerio notariorum et primicerio defensorum tenentibus ei manus, ut communicet eos qui in senatorio sunt, post quem archidiaconus confirmat.

113. When the archdeacon has administered the chalice to those who have received from the pope, the pope comes down from the seat with the chancellor and chief counsellor supporting his hands, in order to give communion to those in the senatorial area. After him, the archdeacon gives them communion under the species of wine.

---

[23] A 'reed' refers to the metal tube, a sort of drinking straw, used at this time for communion from the chalice.

114. Post archidiaconem episcopi communicant et diaconi post eos confirmant.

114. After the archdeacon the bishops give communion, the deacons administer the chalice after them.

115. Nam cum ad communicandum venerit pontifex, antecedit eum acolitus habens sindonem ad collum adpensum, cum qua tenetur patena cum Sancta. Similiter et post diaconos vadunt cum urceis et scyphis fundendo vinum in gemellionibus unde confirmantur populi. Haec faciendo transeunt a dextera in sinistram partem.

115. Now when the pope comes to give communion, an acolyte goes ahead of him with a linen sheet hanging round his neck, with which he holds the paten with the sacrament. Similarly, after the deacons, they go after the deacons with jugs and bowls, pouring the wine into the vessels for the communion of the people.[24] When they do this they go crosswise from right to left.

116. Presbiteri autem, annuente primicerio, iussu pontificis communicant populum et ipsi vicissim confirmant.

116. When the chancellor gives the signal, the presbyters, by the pope's command, give communion to the people and in turn administer the cup.

117. Nam, mox ut pontifex coeperit in senatorio communicare, statim scola incipit antiphonam ad communionem per vices cum subdiaconibus et psallunt usquedum

117. As soon as the pope starts giving communion in the senatorial area, the choir, alternating with the subdeacons, begins the communion antiphon. This continues until

---

[24] The wine collected at the offertory and poured from the chalice into other vessels, has presumably been held somewhere near the altar during the canon of the mass. For the post-medieval sacramental theologian, this might pose the question as to whether it was 'consecrated' or not. Also, there is a great deal of breaking loaves of leavened bread and pouring out and filling small cups ('gemellions') for the communion of the people. This sort of liturgy is not for those inclined to be scrupulous about crumbs or the possible spillage of consecrated elements.

communicato omni populo, annuat pontifex ut dicant 'Gloria patri': et tunc repetito versu quiescunt.

communion has been given to the people. Then, the pope signals to them to sing: 'Glory be to the Father...' and then, having repeated the verse, they stop singing.

118. Nam pontifex, mox ut communicaverit in partes mulierum, redit in sedem et communicat regionarios per ordinem et eos qui in filo steterant. Qui tamen, data statione, ascendunt ad altare. Post pontificem archidiaconus eos confirmat. Pontifex vero, postquam omnes communicaverint, sedet et abluit manus suas.

118. When the pope has given communion in the women's area, he returns to his seat and gives communion to the district officials in order and those who stand in line. These come to the altar, once the next station mass has been announced. After the pope, the archdeacon gives them communion from the cup. Then, after everyone has received communion, the pope sits down and washes his hands.

119. Post omnes hos redeuntes nomincolator et sacellarius et acolytus qui patenam tenet et qui manustergium tenet et qui aquam dat ad sedem communicant.

119. After all these have returned, the secretary and the treasurer and the acolyte who holds the paten and the one who holds the towel and the one who presents the water make their communion at the chair.

120. Post pontificem, archidiaconus eos confirmat.

120. After the pope, the archdeacon administers them the chalice.

121. Adstat autem subdiaconus regionarius ante faciem pontificis, ut

121. The regional subdeacon stands before the pope to receive

annuat ei. Ille vero contemplans populum si iam communicati sunt et annuit ei.

his signal. The pope looks towards the people and if they have finished receiving communion, gives him the signal.

122. Et ille vadit ad humerum, aspicit ad primum scolae, faciens crucem in fronte sua, annuit ei dicere 'Gloriam'; et ille, resalutato, dicit 'Gloria…', 'Sicut erat…', et versum.

122. And he goes to the side of the leader of the schola and making the sign of the cross on his forehead signals to him to sing 'Glory be to the Father…, as it was …' and the antiphon.

123, Finita autem antiphona, surgit pontifex cum archidiacono et veniens ad altare dat orationem ad complendum directus ad orientem; nam in isto loco, cum 'Dominus vobiscum' dixerit, non se dirigit ad populum.

123. When the communion antiphon is over, the pope rises, together with the archdeacon, comes to the altar and recites the prayer after communion facing east, for in the place where he says: 'The Lord be with you' he does not turn to face the people.

124. Finita vero oratione, cui praeceperit archidiaconus de diaconibus aspicit ad pontificem, ut ei annuat, et dicit ad populum: 'Ite missa est'. Resp.: 'Deo gratias'.

124. When the prayer is said, the deacon designated by the archdeacon looks toward the pope so that he may give the signal. He says to the people: 'Go, the mass is ended'. They reply: 'Thanks be to God'.

125. Tunc septem cereostata praecedunt pontificem et subdiaconus cum turibulo ad secretarium.

125. Then the seven candlesticks and the district subdeacon carrying the thurible, precede the pope to the sacristy.

126. Discendente autem ad presbi-

126. As he goes down towards the

terium, episcopi primum dicunt: 'Iube, domne, benedicere'. Respondit: 'Benedicat nos dominus'. Respondunt: 'Amen'; post episcopos presbiteri, deinde monachi, deinde scola, deinde milites draconarii, id est qui signa portant; post eos baiuli; post eos cereostatarii; post quos acolyti qui rugam observant; post eos extra presbiterium cruces portantes, deinde mansionarii iuniores; et intrant in secretarium.

presbyteral area, the bishops first say: 'Master, give a blessing'. He replies: 'May the Lord bless us'. They reply: 'Amen'. After them walk the bishops and presbyters, then the monks, the schola and the standard bearers, those who carry the insignia. After them go the porters, then the candlesticks, after them come the acolytes who watch the gates, then outside the presbyteral area, those who carry the crosses, then the lesser chamberlains. And they enter the sacristy.

Bibliography

Alzati, Cesare, *The Ambrosianum Mysterium: the Church of Milan and its Liturgical Tradition* (2 vols, tr. George Guiver CR, Alcuin/GROW Joint Liturgical Studies 44 and 47–48, Grove Books, Cambridge, 1999 and 2000).

Atchley, E. G. Cuthbert F., *Ordo Romanus Primus, With Introduction and Notes* (The Library of Liturgiology & Ecclesiology For English Readers, Volume vi, Alexander Moring Limited, The De La More Press, London, 1905).

Bishop, Edmund, 'The Genius of the Roman Rite' in E. Bishop, *Studia Liturgica* (The Clarendon Press, Oxford, 1918), pp. 1–19.

Connell, Martin F., *Church and Worship in Fifth Century Rome, The Letter of Innocent I to Decentius of Gubbio* (Alcuin/GROW Joint Liturgical Studies 52, Grove Books, Cambridge, 2002).

Deshusses, Jean (ed.), *Le Sacramentaire Gregorien, Ses Principales Formes D'apres Les Plus Anciens Manuscrits* (3 vols, Editions Universitaires Fribourg Suisse, Fribourg, 1979).

Duchesne, L. (ed), *Le Liber Pontificalis*, 2 vols (Paris, 1886–92) vol. 1 p. 376.

Origines Du Culte Chrétien (5me ed. Paris, 1920) p. 158.

Dumas, A. and Deshusses, J. (eds), *Liber Sacramentorum Gellonensis, textus n.664* (Corpus Christianorum Series Latina 159, Turnhout, Brepols, 1981).

Fagerberg, David, *Theologia Prima, What is Liturgical Theology?* (Liturgy Training Publications, Archdiocese of Chicago, Chicago, 2004).

Fletcher, Richard, *The Conversion of Europe From Paganism to Christianity 371–1386 AD* (Harper Collins, London, 1997).

Griffiths, Alan, *We Give You Thanks and Praise, the Ambrosian Eucharistic Prefaces* (Canterbury Press, London, 1999).

Hen, Yitzhak, *The Royal Patronage of Liturgy in Frankish Gaul* (Henry Bradshaw Society, Subsidia III, London, 2001).

Holland, Tom, *Millennium, The End of the World and the Forging of Christendom* (Abacus, London, 2008).

Jasper, R. C. D. and Cuming, G., *Prayers of the Eucharist, Early and Reformed* (3rd ed. rev. and enlarged, Pueblo, New York, 1987).

Jungmann, Joseph A., SJ, *The Mass of the Roman Rite, its origins and development (Missarum Solemnia)* (2 vols, tr. Rev. Francis A. Brunner, CSSR, reissued by Christian Classics Inc., Westminster, Maryland, 1986).

Kavanagh, Aidan, OSB, *On Liturgical Theology* (Pueblo, New York, 1984).

King, Archdale, *Notes on the Catholic Liturgies* (Longmans, Green and Co., London, 1929).

– *Liturgies of the Primatial Sees* (Longmans, Green and Co., London, 1957).

Lang, Uwe M., *Turning Towards the Lord, Orientation in Liturgical Prayer* (Ignatius Press, San Francisco, 2004).

Legg, J. Wickham (ed.), *The Sarum Missal edited from Three Early Manuscripts* (The Clarendon Press, Oxford, 1916).

Letter, P. De, *Prosper of Aquitaine, Defense of Saint Augustine* (Ancient Christian Writers vol. xxxii, Westminster MD, 1963).

McCall, Richard D., *Liturgy as Performance* (University of Notre Dame Press, Notre Dame, Indiana, 2007).

McClure, Judith and Collins, Roger, *Bede, Ecclesiastical History of the English People, The Greater Chronicle, Bede's Letter to Egbert* (World's Classics Series, Oxford University Press, 1994).

Mohlberg, Leo Cunibert OSB (ed), *Missale Gothicum (Vat. Reg. Lat. 317)* (Casa Editrice, Herder, Rome, 1961).

Mohlberg, Leo Cunibert OSB, Eizenhofer, Leo OSB, and Suffrin, Petrus OSB (eds), *Liber Sacramentorum Romanae Aeclesiae Ordinis Anni Circuli (Cod. Vat. Reg. lat. 316/Paris Bibl. Nat. 7193, 41/56) (Sacramentarium Gelasianum)* (Casa Editrice, Herder, Rome, 1960).

– *Missale Francorum (Cod. Vat. Reg. Lat. 257)* (Casa Editrice, Herder, Rome, 1957).

– *Missale Gallicanum Vetus (Cod. Vat. Palat. Lat. 493)* (Casa Editrice, Herder, Rome, 1958).

– *Sacramentarium Veronense (Cod. Bibl. Capit. Veron. LXXXV[80])* (Casa Editrice, Herder, Rome, 1956).

St Roch, P. (ed), *Liber Sacramentorum Engolismensis (Cod. B.N. Lat.816)* n.650 (Corpus Christianorum Series Latina 159C, Turnhout, Brepols, 1987).

Stringer, Martin D., *A Sociological History of Christian Worship* (Cambridge University Press, Cambridge, 2005).

The Alcuin Club promotes the study of Christian Liturgy, especially the liturgy of the Anglican Communion. It has a long history of publishing an annual Collection, and has shared with GROW since 1987 in also publishing the Joint Liturgical Studies. Members receive all publications free. For membership contact: The Alcuin Club' St Anne's Vicarage, 182 St Ann's Hill, London SW18 2RS. Telephone; 0208 874 2809. E-mail: gordon,jeanes@stanneswandsworth.org.uk

The Group for Renewal of Worship (GROW) has for 40 years been a focus for forward-thinking, often adventurous, explorations in Anglican worship. It has produced (by its own members writing or by its commissioning of others) over 200 titles in the Grove Worship Series, and until 1986 similarly produced Grove Liturgical Studies, many of which are still in print. Enquiries about GROW Grove Books Ltd, Ridley Hall Road, Cambridge CB3 9HU, or to members of the Group.

From 1987 to 2004, the Joint Editorial Board of the two sponsoring agencies commissioned numbers 1–58 of Joint Liturgical Studies, published by Grove Books Ltd (see the Grove Books website or of previous Joint Liturgical Studies). In 2005, 5CM-Canterbury Press Ltd, now Hymns Ancient & Modern, became the publishers. Two titles (of 48–60 pages) are published each year. Available at £6.95 from Hymns Ancient & Modern.

59 (2005) *Proclus on Baptism in Constantinople* by Juliette Day
60 (2005) *1927–28 Prayer Book Crisis in the Church of England Part 1: Ritual, Royal Commission, and Reply to the Royal Letters of Business* by Donald Gray.
61 (2006) *Prayer Book Crisis...Part 2: The cul-de-sac of the 'Deposited Book'...until further notice be taken* by Donald Gray.
62 (2006) *Anglican Swahili Prayer Books* by Ian Tarrant.
63 (2007) *A History of the International Anglican Liturgical Consultations 1983–2007* by David Holeton and Colin Buchanan.
64 (2007) *Justin Martyr on Baptism and Eucharist* edited by Colin Buchanan.
65 (2008) *Anglican Liturgical Identity: Papers from the Prague meeting of the International Anglican Liturgical Consultation* edited by Christopher Irvine.
66 (2008) *The Psalms in Christian Worship: Patristic Precedent and Anglican Practice* by Anthony Gelston.

67 (2009) *Infant Communion from the Reformation to the Present Day* by Mark Dalby.

68 (2009) *The Hampton Court Conference and the 1604 Book of Common Prayer* edited by Colin Buchanan.

69 (2010) *Social Science Methods in Contemporary Liturgical Research: An Introduction* by Trevor Lloyd, James Steven and Phillip Tovey.

70 (2010) *Two Early Egyptian Liturgical Papyri: The Deir Balyzeh Papyrus and the Barcelona Papyrus* translated and edited by Alistair Stewart.

71 (2011) *Anglican Marriage Rites: A symposium* edited by Kenneth W. Stevenson.

72 (2011) *Charles Simeon on The Excellency of the Liturgy* by Andrew Atherstone.

JLS 74 will be the Palermo International Anglican Statement on Funeral Rites with Introduction and supporting Essays.

The current series of Joint Liturgical Studies is available through booksellers, on standing order either by joining the Alcuin Club (see above) or from Hymns Ancient & Modern, Subscription Office, 13a Hellesdon Park Road, Norwich, Norfolk NR6 5DR, UK. Telephone 01603 785910 or online at www.jointliturgicalstudies.co.uk.

CPSIA information can be obtained
at www.ICGtesting.com
Printed in the USA
LVHW081056060321
679151LV00041B/394